Savory Sensations

Delightful Dishes to Elevate Your Everyday Cooking

LAUREL QUINN

The presentation of the information is without contract or any type of guarantee assurance. The trademarks that are used are without any consent, and the publication of the trademark is without permission or backing by the trademark owner. All trademarks and brands within this book are for clarifying purposes only and are the owned by the owners themselves, not affiliated with this document.

Table of Contents

Chapter 1

Introduction

Welcome to Savory Sensations

Welcome to the world of culinary delights, where every meal becomes a journey of flavors and a celebration of taste. This book is your guide to transforming everyday cooking into a series of delightful experiences, making each dish a savory sensation. Whether you are a seasoned cook or a kitchen novice, this collection of recipes and tips will elevate your culinary skills and inspire you to create meals that are not only delicious but also memorable.

Cooking is more than just preparing food; it is an art form that engages all your senses. The vibrant colors of fresh vegetables, the enticing aromas of herbs and spices, the satisfying sizzle of ingredients in a hot pan—all contribute to the magic of cooking. This book is designed to help you harness that magic and bring it into your kitchen, turning routine meals into extraordinary feasts.

To begin your culinary adventure, it is essential to understand the basic principles that underpin great cooking. At the heart of any memorable dish is the quality of its ingredients. Fresh, high-quality ingredients are the foundation of flavorful cooking. Whenever possible, choose seasonal produce, as it is often more flavorful and nutritious. Visit local farmers' markets or specialty stores to find the freshest fruits, vegetables, meats, and seafood. Not only will you be supporting local producers, but you will also be ensuring that your dishes burst with natural flavors.

Another cornerstone of exceptional cooking is mastering essential techniques. From chopping and sautéing to roasting and baking, each technique plays a crucial role in developing flavors and textures. Take the time to practice these techniques, as they will become second nature and allow you to cook with confidence and creativity. For instance, learning how to properly sear meat can make the difference between a bland dish and one that is rich and flavorful. Similarly, mastering the art of making a perfect roux will open up a world of possibilities for creating creamy sauces and soups.

In addition to mastering techniques, understanding the role of seasoning is vital. Salt, pepper, herbs, and spices are the building blocks of flavor. Salt enhances the natural flavors of ingredients, while herbs and spices add complexity and depth. Experiment with different combinations to find your unique flavor profiles. For example, try pairing rosemary with roasted potatoes, or adding a pinch of cumin to your chili. Do not be afraid to experiment and adjust seasonings to suit your taste.

Equally important is the concept of balance in cooking. A well-balanced dish harmonizes various flavors—sweet, salty, sour, bitter, and umami—creating a symphony of taste. Consider the balance of textures as well, combining crunchy, creamy, and tender elements to add interest and satisfaction to your meals. For instance, a salad with crisp greens, creamy avocado, and crunchy nuts offers a delightful contrast of textures, making each bite exciting.

Cooking is also about creativity and personal expression. Do not be afraid to put your spin on traditional recipes or to invent new ones. Use this book as a starting point, but feel free to adapt the recipes to your preferences and dietary needs. Cooking should be a joyful and liberating experience, where you can explore new ingredients, techniques, and cuisines. The more you experiment, the more confident and skilled you will become.

As you embark on this culinary journey, it is helpful to have a well-organized kitchen. A clutter-free, well-stocked kitchen makes cooking more enjoyable and efficient. Keep your pantry stocked with staples such as olive oil, vinegar, grains, and spices. Organize your kitchen tools and equipment so that everything you need is within easy reach. Invest in a few high-quality items, such as a sharp chef's knife, a sturdy cutting board, and reliable cookware. These essentials will make your cooking experience smoother and more pleasurable.

One of the joys of cooking is sharing your creations with others. Whether you are cooking for family, friends, or just for yourself, the act of preparing and enjoying food is a way to connect and create lasting memories. Invite loved ones into your kitchen, involve them in the cooking process, and savor the moments spent together around the table. Cooking and eating together fosters a sense of community and strengthens relationships.

To further enhance your culinary skills, consider exploring different cuisines and cooking styles. Each culture offers unique ingredients, techniques, and flavor combinations that can broaden your culinary horizons. For example, delve into the vibrant world of Italian cooking, with its emphasis on fresh, simple ingredients and bold flavors. Or explore the intricate and aromatic dishes of Indian cuisine, where spices play a central role in creating complex and satisfying meals. By embracing diverse culinary traditions, you will gain a deeper appreciation for the art of cooking and discover new favorites to add to your repertoire.

Cooking is also an opportunity to nourish not just the body, but the soul. Taking the time to prepare a meal with care and intention can be a meditative and fulfilling experience. Focus on the process, savor the aromas and textures, and take pride in the dishes you create. Remember that perfection is not the goal; rather, it is the joy and satisfaction that come from creating something delicious and sharing it with others.

As you move forward with this book, remember that cooking is a continuous learning process. Each recipe you try, each technique you master, and each new ingredient you experiment with adds to your culinary knowledge and skill set. Keep an open mind and a curious palate, always ready to explore and discover.

How to Use This Book

Cooking can be both an art and a science, where each meal is an opportunity to experiment and enjoy the process. This book is designed as your companion in the kitchen, guiding you through a variety of recipes, techniques, and tips to elevate your everyday cooking. To fully benefit from this book, here's how you can use it effectively and make the most of the culinary journey ahead.

Start by familiarizing yourself with the layout and structure of the book. Each chapter is organized to take you through different aspects of cooking, from breakfast delights to impressive dinners and global flavors. The table of contents provides a roadmap to navigate through the sections, allowing you to find specific recipes or techniques based on your needs and interests. Whether you are looking for a quick breakfast idea or planning a special dinner for guests, this book is structured to provide you with a wide range of options.

Before diving into the recipes, take some time to read through the introductory chapters. These sections cover essential cooking tips, techniques, and the basics of stocking your pantry and kitchen. Understanding these fundamentals will set a solid foundation for your cooking endeavors. The advice on kitchen tools and pantry staples, for instance, ensures you have everything you need at your fingertips, making the cooking process smoother and more enjoyable.

As you move on to the recipes, pay attention to the detailed instructions and ingredient lists. Each recipe is crafted to provide clear, step-by-step guidance, making it easy for you to follow along, regardless of your skill level. For beginners, it's helpful to read the entire recipe before starting. This habit allows you to understand the flow of the process and ensures you have all the necessary ingredients and tools ready. For more experienced cooks, feel free to use the recipes as a base and experiment with your variations.

The recipes in this book are designed to be versatile and adaptable. Don't hesitate to make adjustments based on your preferences, dietary restrictions, or ingredient availability. For example, if a recipe calls for a specific type of meat but you prefer a vegetarian option, look for suitable substitutes listed in the book or use your creativity to find alternatives. Flexibility is key to making cooking an enjoyable and personalized experience.

In addition to the recipes, this book includes various cooking techniques and tips that can enhance your skills. Take advantage of these sections to expand your culinary repertoire. Techniques such as proper knife handling, sautéing, and roasting are fundamental skills that will improve your efficiency and confidence in the kitchen. Practice these techniques regularly, and soon they will become second nature, allowing you to tackle more complex recipes with ease.

To get the most out of the global flavors chapter, approach each cuisine with an open mind and a spirit of adventure. Trying dishes from different cultures not only broadens your taste horizons but also introduces you to new ingredients and cooking methods. These experiences can inspire you to incorporate diverse flavors into your everyday cooking, making your meals more exciting and varied. Pay attention to the unique spices and herbs used in each cuisine and experiment with incorporating them into your dishes.

Meal planning is another aspect where this book can be incredibly useful. By exploring different chapters, you can plan your meals for the week, ensuring a balanced and varied diet. Start by selecting recipes from different sections—breakfast, lunch, and dinner—to create a comprehensive meal plan. This approach saves time and reduces the stress of last-minute cooking decisions. Additionally, having a meal plan helps in creating a shopping list, ensuring you have all the necessary ingredients on hand.

If you are cooking for a family or entertaining guests, use the book to find recipes that cater to various tastes and dietary needs. Many recipes include suggestions for modifications to accommodate different preferences, such as vegetarian or gluten-free options. By preparing a variety of dishes, you can ensure that everyone at the table finds something they enjoy.

Cooking is not just about following recipes; it's also about developing your intuition and creativity. Use the tips and techniques in this book as a starting point, and don't be afraid to experiment. Trust your senses—taste, smell, and sight—to guide you. If something doesn't turn out as expected, view it as a learning experience rather than a failure. Each mistake is an opportunity to refine your skills and improve.

To keep track of your progress and preferences, consider keeping a cooking journal. Note down the recipes you've tried, any modifications you made, and how the dish turned out. This practice helps you remember what worked well and what didn't, making it easier to recreate successful dishes in the future. Over time, you'll build a personalized collection of recipes and tips that reflect your culinary journey.

Finally, remember that cooking is meant to be a joyful and rewarding experience. Don't rush through the process; take the time to savor each step. Engage your senses and enjoy the act of creating something delicious. Share your culinary creations with family and friends, and relish the moments spent together around the table.

This book is more than just a collection of recipes; it's a guide to discovering the joy of cooking and the satisfaction of creating meals that delight the senses. By using this book thoughtfully and intentionally, you can transform your kitchen into a place of creativity and pleasure.

Essential Cooking Tips and Techniques

Mastering essential cooking tips and techniques can transform your kitchen endeavors from daunting to delightful. Understanding these basics not only enhances your skills but also boosts your confidence, allowing you to tackle recipes with ease and creativity.

One of the most fundamental skills in cooking is proper knife handling. A sharp knife is crucial for safety and efficiency. Dull knives require more force and are more likely to slip and cause injuries. Learn to hold your knife correctly: grip the handle with your dominant hand and place your thumb and index finger on either side of the blade for control. Practice basic cuts such as dicing, slicing, and chopping. Ensure your cutting board is stable by placing a damp cloth underneath it to prevent slipping. Mastering these knife skills will save you time and make food preparation smoother.

Seasoning is another critical aspect of cooking. Salt enhances the natural flavors of food, while a variety of herbs and spices can add depth and complexity. Understanding when and how to season can make or break a dish. For instance, seasoning meat before cooking allows the salt to penetrate and enhance the flavor, while adding fresh herbs at the end preserves their delicate taste. Experiment with different spices and herbs to find combinations that you enjoy. A well-seasoned dish can turn a simple meal into a culinary delight.

Temperature control is essential for achieving the desired results in cooking. Whether you're searing a steak, baking bread, or simmering a sauce, the right temperature can make all the difference. For stovetop cooking, learn to use high heat for searing and lower heat for simmering and gentle cooking. When baking, always preheat your oven to the required temperature before placing your dish inside. Use a meat thermometer to check for doneness, especially with roasts and poultry, to ensure they're cooked through without being overdone.

Another key technique is the concept of mise en place, a French term meaning "everything in its place." This involves preparing and organizing all your ingredients before you start cooking. Measure out spices, chop vegetables, and have all your tools at hand. This practice not only makes the cooking process more efficient but also helps you avoid mistakes and ensures you don't forget any ingredients. Mise end place is particularly useful when following complex recipes or cooking multiple dishes simultaneously.

Understanding the different cooking methods is crucial. Each technique brings out unique flavors and textures in food. Sautéing is a quick method for cooking small pieces of food in a hot pan with a small amount of oil. It's perfect for vegetables, chicken strips, or shrimp. Roasting, on the other hand, uses dry heat to cook food evenly and develop a rich, caramelized exterior. It's ideal for meats and root vegetables. Grilling adds a smoky flavor and is great for meats, vegetables, and even fruits. Steaming preserves nutrients and is excellent for delicate foods like fish and greens. Experiment with these methods to discover how they affect the taste and texture of your dishes.

Timing is another crucial element in cooking. Overcooking or undercooking can ruin a dish. Pay attention to cooking times in recipes, but also learn to trust your senses. Visual cues, such as the color of a crust or the firmness of a vegetable, can help you determine doneness. Practice makes perfect, so the more you cook, the better you'll become at gauging cooking times.

Deglazing is a technique that involves adding liquid to a hot pan to scrape up the flavorful browned bits stuck to the bottom. This method is often used to make sauces after sautéing meat or vegetables. Wine, broth, or even water can be used to deglaze a pan. The resulting sauce can then be reduced and seasoned to taste. Deglazing adds depth and richness to sauces and gravies, making them more flavorful and complex.

Emulsification is another important technique, particularly in making dressings and sauces. It involves combining two liquids that normally don't mix, such as oil and vinegar. To create a stable emulsion, slowly whisk the oil into the vinegar while constantly stirring. This process can also be done in a blender or food processor. Emulsified sauces, like mayonnaise or vinaigrette, have a smooth, creamy texture that enhances salads and sandwiches.

Resting meat after cooking is a tip often overlooked but crucial for juicy, tender results. When you cook meat, the juices are driven to the center. Letting the meat rest allows the juices to redistribute throughout, making it more moist and flavorful. As a rule of thumb, smaller cuts need about five minutes of rest, while larger roasts might need up to 20 minutes.

Baking requires precision and patience. Unlike cooking, where you can often adjust ingredients on the fly, baking is more of a science. Accurate measurements are key. Use a kitchen scale for the best results, as it provides more precision than volume measurements. Pay attention to the order of ingredients and mixing techniques. Overmixing can develop too much gluten, leading to dense, tough baked goods. Following instructions carefully ensures consistent and delicious results.

Making homemade stocks is an excellent way to enhance your cooking and reduce waste. Save vegetable scraps, bones, and meat trimmings in your freezer. When you have enough, simmer them with water, herbs, and spices to create a flavorful stock. Strain and store it in portions for future use in soups, sauces, and stews. Homemade stock adds depth and richness that store-bought versions often lack, and it's a great way to make the most of your ingredients.

Stocking Your Pantry

A well-stocked pantry is the cornerstone of efficient and enjoyable cooking. Having the right ingredients on hand can make meal preparation smoother, inspire creativity, and ensure you're always ready to whip up something delicious. Let's explore how to stock your pantry with essentials that cater to a variety of dishes and culinary needs.

Start with the basics: grains, pasta, and legumes. These staples are versatile and form the foundation of many meals. Keep a variety of grains such as rice (white, brown, and basmati), quinoa, and barley. Each has unique textures and flavors that complement different dishes. For instance, quinoa is a great protein-rich option for salads, while basmati rice pairs beautifully with Indian and Middle Eastern cuisines. Pasta is another must-have, with types like spaghetti, penne, and fusilli offering different shapes for various sauces and preparations. Legumes, including lentils, chickpeas, and black beans, are essential for adding protein and fiber to soups, stews, and salads.

Flours and baking essentials should also have a dedicated spot in your pantry. All-purpose flour is the most versatile, but consider having whole wheat, bread flour, and pastry flour for specific baking needs. Stock up on baking powder, baking soda, yeast, and cornstarch. These ingredients are crucial for everything from baking to thickening sauces and gravies. Sugar is another essential, with granulated sugar, brown sugar, and powdered sugar each serving different purposes in your baking repertoire.

Oils and vinegars are indispensable for cooking and dressing salads. Olive oil is a staple, ideal for cooking and as a finishing oil. Vegetable oil or canola oil is great for high-heat cooking and frying. Consider specialty oils like sesame oil for Asian dishes or walnut oil for a nutty flavor in salads. Vinegars, such as white wine vinegar, balsamic vinegar, apple cider vinegar, and rice vinegar, add acidity and depth to your dishes. Each type of vinegar has a unique flavor profile that can enhance different recipes.

Canned goods are lifesavers for quick and easy meals. Keep a variety of canned tomatoes (diced, crushed, and whole) for sauces, soups, and stews. Canned beans, such as kidney beans, cannellini beans, and black beans, are perfect for adding protein and fiber to dishes without the long cooking time. Tuna, sardines, and salmon are excellent sources of protein and can be used in salads, sandwiches, and casseroles. Coconut milk is a versatile ingredient for curries, soups, and desserts, adding a rich, creamy texture and flavor.

Spices and herbs are the heart of flavorful cooking. Basic spices like salt, pepper, paprika, cumin, coriander, and chili powder should always be within reach. Fresh herbs can be a game-changer, but dried herbs like oregano, thyme, rosemary, and bay leaves are also essential. Ground spices like cinnamon, nutmeg, and cloves are perfect for both savory dishes and baking. Whole spices, such as cumin seeds, mustard seeds, and cardamom pods, are great for toasting and grinding fresh for more intense flavors. Don't forget to stock up on specialty spices based on your preferred cuisines, such as garam masala for Indian dishes or five-spice powder for Chinese cooking.

Condiments and sauces add instant flavor and variety to your meals. Soy sauce, fish sauce, and oyster sauce are staples for Asian cuisine. Worcestershire sauce and hot sauce can enhance everything from soups to marinades. Dijon mustard, whole grain mustard, and mayonnaise are versatile ingredients for dressings and sandwiches. Honey and maple syrup are natural sweeteners that also work well in marinades and glazes.

Broths and stocks are crucial for soups, stews, and sauces. Keep chicken, beef, and vegetable broth on hand, either in cartons, cans, or homemade and frozen. They add depth and richness to dishes and can be used as a cooking liquid for grains and legumes to infuse extra flavor.

Nuts, seeds, and dried fruits are not only great for snacking but also for adding texture and flavor to dishes. Almonds, walnuts, and cashews can be used in salads, granola, and baking. Seeds like chia, flax, and pumpkin are excellent for adding nutritional value to smoothies, oatmeal, and baked goods. Dried fruits, such as raisins, cranberries, and apricots, offer natural sweetness and chewiness to salads, pilafs, and desserts.

Keeping a variety of cooking wines and spirits can elevate your cooking. Dry white wine and red wine are often used in sauces and stews. Vermouth is great for deglazing pans, and sherry adds a unique depth to soups and sauces. Don't overlook the role of spirits like brandy, rum, and bourbon, which can be used in both savory dishes and desserts to add complex flavors.

Storage solutions are just as important as the ingredients themselves. Use airtight containers to keep ingredients fresh and prevent pests. Glass jars are excellent for storing grains, pasta, and legumes, allowing you to see what you have at a glance. Label each container with the name and date to keep track of freshness, especially for items like flours and nuts, which can go rancid over time. Stackable containers and baskets can help maximize space in your pantry and keep everything organized.

Kitchen Tools You Need

Equipping your kitchen with the right tools is essential for cooking efficiency and enjoyment. With a well-chosen arsenal of utensils, gadgets, and appliances, you can tackle a wide range of recipes and cooking techniques. Here's a comprehensive guide to the kitchen tools you need to transform your culinary space into a functional and inspiring haven.

Start with quality knives. A chef's knife is you're most important tool, versatile enough for chopping vegetables, slicing meat, and mincing herbs. Invest in a high-quality chef's knife with a comfortable handle and a sharp, durable blade. Complement it with a paring knife for more delicate tasks like peeling fruit and a serrated bread knife for slicing through crusty loaves. Regularly hone and occasionally sharpen your knives to maintain their edge and ensure safe, efficient cutting.

Cutting boards are the next crucial component. Have at least two: one for raw meats and another for fruits, vegetables, and other ready-to-eat foods to prevent cross-contamination. Wooden cutting boards are gentle on knives and provide a sturdy surface, while plastic boards are easier to sanitize. A small cutting board can also be handy for quick tasks, like slicing a lemon.

Measuring tools are indispensable for both precise cooking and baking. Measuring cups and spoons are essential for dry and liquid ingredients. Look for sturdy, easy-to-read sets that include a variety of sizes. A kitchen scale is also invaluable, particularly for baking, where accuracy is key. With a scale, you can measure ingredients by weight, ensuring consistency and precision.

Mixing bowls in various sizes are necessary for preparing and combining ingredients. Stainless steel bowls are durable and versatile, while glass bowls are microwave-safe and allow you to see the contents easily. Nesting bowls save space and offer convenient storage.

A set of pots and pans forms the backbone of your cooking endeavors. At a minimum, you'll need a large pot for boiling pasta, making soup, and other large-volume tasks; a medium saucepan for sauces and reheating; and a small saucepan for smaller quantities and delicate sauces. For frying, sautéing, and searing, a versatile frying pan or skillet is essential. Nonstick pans are great for eggs and other delicate foods, while cast iron skillets provide excellent heat retention and can go from stovetop to oven.

Baking sheets and pans are necessary for a variety of tasks beyond just baking. A sturdy baking sheet can be used for roasting vegetables, baking cookies, and even making sheet pan dinners. Have at least one rimmed baking sheet to prevent spills. A muffin tin, loaf pan, and cake pans (round and square) are also useful for baking a variety of goods.

Utensils are the workhorses of the kitchen. A good set should include a spatula, tongs, wooden spoons, a slotted spoon, and a ladle. Silicone spatulas are heat-resistant and flexible, perfect for scraping bowls and folding batters. Tongs are indispensable for flipping meats and serving salads. Wooden spoons are gentle on nonstick surfaces and ideal for stirring and mixing. A slotted spoon is perfect for lifting items out of liquid, and a ladle is essential for serving soups and stews.

A colander or strainer is necessary for draining pasta, rinsing vegetables, and other tasks. A large colander is versatile for most needs, but having a fine-mesh strainer can be useful for more delicate tasks like sifting flour or straining sauces.

Small appliances can significantly enhance your kitchen's functionality. A blender or food processor is invaluable for making smoothies, soups, sauces, and more. Choose a high-powered model for versatility and durability. An immersion blender is a convenient tool for pureeing soups directly in the pot and making quick emulsifications. A stand mixer can be a game-changer for baking, making tasks like kneading bread dough and whipping cream much easier.

Storage containers are essential for keeping your ingredients fresh and organized. Glass or plastic containers with airtight lids are ideal for leftovers, meal prep, and storing pantry staples. Look for stackable containers to save space and ensure your pantry and fridge remain orderly.

A few specialized tools can elevate your cooking experience. A micro plane or zester is perfect for grating citrus zest, hard cheeses, and spices like nutmeg. A mandolin slicer can make quick work of slicing vegetables uniformly, essential for dishes like gratins and salads. A peeler is another small but vital tool, making it easy to remove the skins from fruits and vegetables.

Thermometers are crucial for ensuring food safety and perfect cooking results. An instant-read thermometer helps you check the internal temperature of meats, bread, and other cooked foods, ensuring they are cooked to the proper level. An oven thermometer can help you verify that your oven is heating accurately, which is important for baking.

Timers and thermometers aren't the only tech tools that can enhance your kitchen. A digital scale is another gadget that can bring a high level of precision to your cooking and baking. For the tech-savvy cook, a smart speaker or a tablet with a sturdy stand can be a helpful addition, allowing you to follow recipes hands-free, set multiple timers, and even play music or podcasts while you cook.

Chapter 2

Breakfast Bliss

Energizing Smoothies and Juices

Smoothies and juices can be a game-changer when it comes to energizing your mornings and infusing your day with essential nutrients. They offer a quick, delicious, and versatile way to consume a variety of fruits, vegetables, and other healthy ingredients. Whether you're looking to boost your energy, improve your digestion, or simply enjoy a refreshing drink, mastering the art of making smoothies and juices can transform your health routine.

The beauty of smoothies lies in their simplicity and adaptability. At their core, smoothies are a blend of fruits, vegetables, liquids, and often additional ingredients like yogurt, nuts, seeds, or protein powders. The key to a perfect smoothie is balance. A good smoothie has a harmonious blend of flavors and a creamy texture without being too thick or too watery.

Start with a liquid base. Water, milk (dairy or plant-based), and fruit juices are popular choices. Coconut water is a fantastic option for its hydrating properties and subtle sweetness. For a creamier texture, try almond milk, oat milk, or even a splash of coconut milk. The liquid you choose can greatly influence the flavor and nutritional profile of your smoothie.

Next, add your fruits. Bananas are a common choice as they add natural sweetness and a creamy texture.

Berries, such as strawberries, blueberries, and raspberries, are high in antioxidants and provide vibrant color and tartness. Mangoes, pineapples, and peaches can give your smoothie a tropical twist. Remember, frozen fruits can be just as nutritious as fresh ones and provide a thicker consistency.

Incorporating vegetables is a smart way to boost the nutritional value of your smoothie without compromising on taste. Spinach and kale are popular choices because they blend well and have a mild flavor. Carrots and cucumbers add refreshing notes and additional vitamins. Don't be afraid to experiment with other greens like Swiss chard or beet greens to see what you enjoy.

Protein is essential for keeping you full and energized, especially if your smoothie is replacing a meal. Greek yogurt, cottage cheese, or a scoop of protein powder can add a substantial protein boost. Plant-based protein sources like almond butter, chia seeds, hemp seeds, and silken tofu are excellent alternatives. These not only provide protein but also healthy fats and fiber.

Speaking of healthy fats, they are crucial for satiety and nutrient absorption. Avocado, nuts, and seeds can provide the fats you need. A tablespoon of flaxseed or chia seeds can add omega-3 fatty acids, which are beneficial for heart health. Nut butters like almond or peanut butter can make your smoothie more indulgent while adding protein and fats.

Sweeteners are often unnecessary if you use ripe fruits, but if you prefer a sweeter taste, opt for natural sweeteners. A drizzle of honey, maple syrup, or agave nectar can enhance the flavor without the need for refined sugars. Dates are another excellent natural sweetener and also add fiber.

Spices and herbs can elevate your smoothie to the next level. A dash of cinnamon, nutmeg, or vanilla extract can add warmth and complexity. Fresh herbs like mint or basil can provide a refreshing twist. Ginger and turmeric are fantastic for their anti-inflammatory properties and can add a zing to your drink.

To ensure smooth blending, it's important to layer your ingredients properly. Liquids should go in first, followed by softer ingredients like yogurt or nut butter, then leafy greens, and finally, frozen fruits and ice. This method helps the blades move freely and blend everything uniformly.

Juices, on the other hand, offer a different set of benefits. They are typically lighter and can be an excellent way to hydrate and get a quick infusion of vitamins and minerals. Unlike smoothies, juices remove the fiber from fruits and vegetables, making the nutrients more quickly absorbable.

A good juicer is essential for making fresh, high-quality juice. Centrifugal juicers are fast and efficient, making them great for harder fruits and vegetables. Masticating juicers, also known as cold-press juicers, operate more slowly but are excellent for leafy greens and preserving nutrients.

When making juices, start with a base of high-water content fruits or vegetables. Cucumbers and celery are great foundational ingredients due to their mild flavor and high water content. Apples and pears add sweetness and can help balance stronger flavors from greens.

Greens are a powerhouse of nutrients but can have a strong taste. Spinach and romaine lettuce are milder and blend well with other ingredients. Kale, Swiss chard, and parsley are more robust and can be balanced with sweeter fruits.

Citrus fruits like oranges, lemons, and limes can add brightness and acidity to your juice. They are also high in vitamin C, which is excellent for your immune system. Pineapple and grapefruit can also provide a tangy sweetness that complements greens well.

Root vegetables like carrots and beets are fantastic for juicing. Carrots are naturally sweet and rich in beta-carotene, which is good for your eyes and skin. Beets have an earthy flavor and are packed with antioxidants and nitrates that can help improve blood flow and lower blood pressure. When juicing root vegetables, remember that a little goes a long way due to their dense nutrient content and strong flavors.

Classic and Creative Egg Dishes

Eggs have long been a staple in kitchens worldwide, celebrated for their versatility, affordability, and nutritional value. From classic preparations to innovative culinary creations, eggs can be transformed into a myriad of delightful dishes. This chapter will guide you through a variety of both timeless and inventive egg recipes, providing practical tips and techniques to elevate your cooking.

One of the most beloved ways to enjoy eggs is through the classic scrambled eggs. Achieving the perfect scramble requires attention to detail and a few key steps. Start with fresh eggs, cracking them into a bowl and whisking thoroughly until the yolks and whites are completely combined. This ensures an even texture. Adding a splash of milk or cream can create a creamier consistency, while a pinch of salt at this stage helps to enhance the flavor.

Heat a non-stick skillet over medium-low heat and add a pat of butter, allowing it to melt and coat the pan evenly. Pour in the egg mixture and let it sit undisturbed for a few moments. Using a spatula, gently stir the eggs, pushing them from the edges toward the center. This technique creates soft, fluffy curds. Remove the eggs from the heat just before they are fully set, as residual heat will continue to cook them to perfection.

For a more indulgent twist, consider making French-style scrambled eggs, or "oeufs brouillés." These are cooked slowly over very low heat, with constant stirring, resulting in a custard-like texture. Adding a dollop of crème fraiche or a bit of cream at the end creates an exquisite richness. Serve them on toasted brioche or with smoked salmon for a luxurious breakfast or brunch.

Omelets offer endless possibilities for customization, making them a favorite for many. The key to a great omelet lies in its preparation. Begin by whisking eggs with a pinch of salt and a splash of water, which helps to create steam and a lighter texture. Heat a non-stick skillet over medium-high heat and add a small amount of butter, swirling it to coat the pan.

Pour in the egg mixture and let it cook undisturbed for a few seconds until the edges start to set. Using a spatula, gently lift the edges and tilt the pan to allow uncooked eggs to flow underneath. Once the eggs are mostly set but still slightly runny on top, add your desired fillings. Classic choices include cheese, ham, mushrooms, and bell peppers, but don't be afraid to get creative with ingredients like goat cheese, sun-dried tomatoes, or fresh herbs.

Fold the omelet in half or roll it into a cylinder, then slide it onto a plate. The residual heat will finish cooking the eggs and melt the cheese, resulting in a perfectly cooked omelet with a luscious interior. For a touch of elegance, garnish with a sprinkle of chives or a drizzle of truffle oil.

Poached eggs are another classic preparation that can elevate a simple dish to something extraordinary. The key to successful poaching is using fresh eggs, as older eggs tend to spread out too much in the water. Fill a shallow saucepan with water and bring it to a gentle simmer. Adding a splash of vinegar helps the egg whites to coagulate more quickly.

Crack an egg into a small bowl or ramekin, then create a gentle whirlpool in the simmering water using a spoon. Carefully slide the egg into the center of the whirlpool, which helps to keep the whites together. Let the egg cook undisturbed for about three minutes for a runny yolk or a bit longer for a firmer texture. Use a slotted spoon to remove the egg and drain it on a paper towel.

Poached eggs are the star of many classic dishes, such as Eggs Benedict. This luxurious brunch favorite consists of a toasted English muffin topped with Canadian bacon, a poached egg, and a generous drizzle of hollandaise sauce. To make hollandaise, whisk together egg yolks, lemon juice, and a pinch of salt in a heatproof bowl set over simmering water. Slowly drizzle in melted butter while whisking continuously until the sauce is thickened and emulsified. Season with a touch of cayenne pepper or a dash of white wine vinegar for added complexity.

For a creative twist on poached eggs, try serving them over a bed of sautéed spinach and mushrooms, or on top of a spicy avocado toast. The rich, runny yolk adds a luxurious touch to any dish and pairs well with a variety of flavors.

Baked eggs, or "shakshuka," offer a hearty and flavorful option for breakfast, brunch, or even dinner. Originating from North Africa, shakshuka features eggs poached in a spicy tomato sauce. To prepare, sauté onions, bell peppers, and garlic in olive oil until softened. Add tomatoes, tomato paste, and a blend of spices such as cumin, paprika, and chili powder. Simmer the sauce until thickened, then create small wells with a spoon and crack an egg into each well.

Cover the skillet and let the eggs cook until the whites are set but the yolks remain runny. Garnish with fresh herbs like cilantro or parsley and serve with crusty bread or warm pita for dipping. Shakshuka is highly adaptable; consider adding ingredients like crumbled feta, olives, or even chorizo to customize the dish to your taste.

Pancakes, Waffles, and French toast

Few breakfast dishes evoke the same sense of comfort and indulgence as pancakes, waffles, and French toast. These classics have graced our morning tables for generations, each offering a unique texture and flavor profile. Whether you're preparing a relaxed weekend breakfast or an elaborate brunch spread, mastering the art of these beloved dishes can elevate your culinary repertoire and delight your guests.

Pancakes are perhaps the most iconic of the trio, known for their fluffy texture and golden-brown exterior. The foundation of great pancakes lies in a well-balanced batter. To start, combine flour, sugar, baking powder, and a pinch of salt in a large bowl. These dry ingredients provide structure, sweetness, and leavening. In a separate bowl, whisk together milk, eggs, and melted butter. The key to fluffy pancakes is to combine the wet and dry ingredients gently, just until combined. Overmixing can lead to tough, dense pancakes.

For a classic buttermilk pancake, substitute buttermilk for regular milk. The acidity of the buttermilk reacts with the baking powder, producing extra lift and a tender crumb. Once your batter is ready, heat a griddle or non-stick skillet over medium heat and lightly grease it with butter or oil. Pour the batter onto the griddle using a ladle or measuring cup, creating evenly sized circles. Cook until bubbles form on the surface and the edges look set, then flip and cook until golden brown on the other side.

Pancakes are endlessly customizable. For a fruity twist, add fresh blueberries or sliced bananas to the batter. Chocolate chips or nuts can introduce a delightful texture and sweetness. Experimenting with different flours, such as whole wheat or almond flour, can also add nutritional value and unique flavors.

Waffles, with their crisp exterior and tender interior, offer a different texture experience from pancakes. The secret to exceptional waffles lies in the batter and the waffle iron. Begin by whisking together flour, sugar, baking powder, and salt in one bowl. In another, mix milk, eggs, melted butter, and vanilla extract. For an extra touch of decadence, you can fold in whipped egg whites, which helps to create an airy, light texture.

Preheat your waffle iron and lightly grease it with non-stick spray or butter. Pour the batter into the center of the iron, using enough to cover most of the surface without overflowing. Close the iron and cook according to the manufacturer's instructions, usually for about 3-5 minutes, until the waffles are golden brown and crisp. The waffle's distinct grid pattern is perfect for holding syrup, fruit, or whipped cream.

Belgian waffles, known for their deeper pockets and lighter texture, are a popular variant. They typically use yeast in the batter, which requires a bit of patience but rewards you with a wonderfully airy waffle. Combine warm milk, sugar, and yeast, letting it sit until bubbly. Mix in flour, melted butter, and beaten eggs, then allow the batter to rise for about an hour. The result is a waffle with a slightly tangy flavor and an incredibly light texture.

French toast, often considered the most luxurious of the three, transforms simple bread into a rich and custardy delight. The key to perfect French toast is choosing the right bread. Thick slices of brioche, challah, or even a sturdy country loaf work best, as they can absorb the custard mixture without falling apart.

Begin by whisking together eggs, milk, a touch of sugar, and a splash of vanilla extract in a shallow dish. For an added layer of flavor, you can include a pinch of cinnamon or nutmeg. Dip each slice of bread into the mixture, allowing it to soak up the custard without becoming too soggy.

Heat a skillet or griddle over medium heat and melt a generous amount of butter. Cook the soaked bread slices until golden brown on each side, about 3-4 minutes per side. The result should be a crisp exterior with a soft, creamy interior. Serve French toast with a dusting of powdered sugar, a drizzle of maple syrup, and fresh berries for a classic presentation.

For a more decadent variation, consider stuffing your French toast. Spread a layer of cream cheese, Nutella, or fruit preserves between two slices of bread before dipping them into the custard mixture. Cook as usual, and you'll have a delightful surprise inside each bite.

Pancakes, waffles, and French toast are not only breakfast staples but also blank canvases for creativity. Consider incorporating seasonal ingredients to make the most of fresh produce. In the fall, add a touch of pumpkin puree and spices like cinnamon and nutmeg to your pancake or waffle batter. During the summer, top your French toast with macerated berries and a dollop of whipped cream.

Savory versions of these dishes can be equally satisfying. For savory pancakes, reduce the sugar in the batter and add ingredients like grated cheese, chopped herbs, or cooked bacon. Serve with a dollop of sour cream and a sprinkle of chives. Savory waffles can be made by incorporating shredded cheese, cooked bacon, and even finely chopped vegetables into the batter. These waffles pair wonderfully with fried chicken for a classic Southern dish or can be served with a poached egg and hollandaise sauce for a savory brunch treat.

Healthy Breakfast Bowls

A healthy breakfast bowl is more than just a nutritious start to your day; it's an opportunity to be creative, to enjoy vibrant flavors, and to fuel your body with the energy it needs. Breakfast bowls can be tailored to suit any dietary preference, whether you're vegan, gluten-free, or simply looking to incorporate more whole foods into your diet. They are versatile, easy to prepare, and can be as simple or as elaborate as you desire.

One of the most popular types of breakfast bowls is the smoothie bowl. The foundation of a smoothie bowl is a thick, creamy blend of fruits and vegetables. Start with a base of frozen fruits like bananas, berries, or mangoes. These provide natural sweetness and a creamy texture. Adding leafy greens such as spinach or kale boosts the nutrient content without overpowering the flavor. For added creaminess and healthy fats, blend in avocado or a spoonful of nut butter.

To create a smoothie bowl, combine your chosen fruits and vegetables in a blender with a splash of liquid. Almond milk, coconut water, or even plain water can be used, depending on your preference. The key is to use just enough liquid to blend the ingredients smoothly while keeping the mixture thick. Pour the smoothie into a bowl and top with an array of toppings. Fresh fruits, granola, nuts, seeds, and shredded coconut are all excellent choices. These toppings not only add texture and flavor but also provide additional nutrients.

Another delicious option is the yogurt bowl. Using Greek yogurt as a base provides a creamy and protein-rich foundation. Greek yogurt is thicker and contains more protein than regular yogurt, making it an excellent choice for a filling breakfast. If you prefer a dairy-free option, coconut yogurt or almond milk yogurt are great alternatives.

To assemble a yogurt bowl, start with a generous scoop of yogurt in your bowl. Add a variety of toppings to enhance the flavor and nutritional value. Fresh fruits like berries, kiwi, and banana slices add natural sweetness and vitamins. Nuts and seeds provide crunch and healthy fats, while a drizzle of honey or maple syrup can add a touch of sweetness. For an extra boost of nutrients, sprinkle on some chia seeds, flaxseeds, or hemp seeds. These tiny powerhouses are rich in omega-3 fatty acids, fiber, and antioxidants.

Overnight oats are another fantastic breakfast bowl option, especially for those with busy mornings. This no-cook method involves soaking oats in liquid overnight, resulting in a creamy and ready-to-eat breakfast by morning. To make overnight oats, combine rolled oats with your choice of milk in a jar or bowl. Almond milk, soy milk, and coconut milk are popular choices, but any milk will work. The ratio is typically one part oats to one part liquid, but you can adjust based on your preferred consistency.

Add-ins can transform basic overnight oats into a flavorful and nutrient-dense meal. Consider stirring in a spoonful of chia seeds, which will absorb liquid and create a pudding-like texture. Sweeten the mixture with a bit of honey, maple syrup, or mashed banana. You can also mix in spices like cinnamon or nutmeg for added flavor. Seal the container and refrigerate overnight. In the morning, give the oats a good stir and top with fresh fruits, nuts, and seeds.

For a savory twist on breakfast bowls, consider a grain bowl. These bowls often use whole grains like quinoa, farro, or brown rice as the base. These grains are rich in fiber, protein, and essential nutrients, making them a hearty and satisfying option. Cooking the grains ahead of time and storing them in the refrigerator makes assembly quick and easy in the morning.

To build a savory grain bowl, start with a scoop of your chosen grain. Add a variety of colorful vegetables for a nutrient boost. Roasted sweet potatoes, sautéed greens, and avocado slices are excellent choices. For protein, consider adding a poached egg, tofu, or chickpeas. Drizzle with a flavorful sauce or dressing, such as tahini, avocado dressing, or a simple olive oil and lemon juice mix. Fresh herbs like cilantro, parsley, or basil can add a burst of flavor and freshness.

Chia pudding bowls offer another nutritious and versatile breakfast option. Chia seeds are rich in omega-3 fatty acids, fiber, and protein, and when soaked in liquid, they expand and form a gel-like consistency. To make chia pudding, combine chia seeds with your choice of milk in a jar or bowl. The typical ratio is three tablespoons of chia seeds to one cup of liquid, but you can adjust based on your preferred thickness.

Sweeten the mixture with a bit of honey, maple syrup, or vanilla extract. Stir well to ensure the seeds are evenly distributed, then refrigerate for at least a few hours or overnight. The chia seeds will absorb the liquid and thicken into a pudding-like texture. In the morning, give the pudding a good stir and top with fresh fruits, nuts, seeds, and a sprinkle of granola for added crunch.

For those who enjoy a hot breakfast, a warm porridge bowl can be a comforting and nutritious option. Porridge can be made from a variety of grains, including oats, quinoa, millet, or amaranth. Oats, particularly steel-cut or rolled oats, are a popular choice due to their creamy texture and numerous health benefits. They are rich in fiber, which aids digestion and helps keep you feeling full throughout the morning.

Quick Breads and Muffins

Quick breads and muffins are delightful additions to any baker's repertoire, offering the convenience of being both easy to make and highly customizable. Unlike traditional bread, which relies on yeast and lengthy rising times, quick breads use baking powder or baking soda as leavening agents. This method allows for a much faster preparation, making them perfect for busy mornings or spontaneous baking sessions.

Think of the classic banana bread, a staple in many kitchens. It starts with ripe bananas, mashed to a smooth consistency. These bananas not only add natural sweetness but also moisture, which is essential for a tender crumb. The beauty of banana bread lies in its simplicity; basic ingredients like flour, sugar, eggs, and a leavening agent come together quickly. Yet, it offers ample room for creativity. You might add a handful of walnuts for crunch, or perhaps some chocolate chips for a touch of indulgence. The key is to not overmix the batter. Overmixing can lead to a dense, tough loaf, so stir just until the ingredients are combined.

Zucchini bread is another beloved variation. Here, grated zucchini imparts moisture and a subtle vegetal note that pairs wonderfully with warm spices like cinnamon and nutmeg. It's an excellent way to use up an abundance of summer zucchini and sneak some extra vegetables into your diet. As with banana bread, the trick lies in balancing the wet and dry ingredients to achieve a moist but not soggy texture.

Muffins, the pint-sized cousins of quick breads, follow a similar principle but offer the advantage of individual portions. Blueberry muffins, for instance, can brighten up any breakfast with their burst of juicy berries and tender crumb. Fresh or frozen blueberries work equally well, though it's advisable to toss them in a bit of flour before folding them into the batter. This trick prevents the berries from sinking to the bottom and ensures an even distribution.

In making muffins, the muffin method is often employed. This involves mixing the wet ingredients in one bowl and the dry ingredients in another before combining them. The goal is to minimize gluten development, which can make the muffins tough. A few lumps in the batter are perfectly fine and even desirable. Once the batter is ready, scoop it into a lined muffin tin, filling each cup about two-thirds full. This allows room for the muffins to rise without overflowing.

Cornbread, a staple of Southern cuisine, offers a savory take on quick bread. Made primarily with cornmeal, it boasts a unique texture and flavor. Traditional recipes might include buttermilk for tanginess and a bit of sugar for balance. Cornbread is incredibly versatile: it pairs beautifully with chili, can be enjoyed on its own, or even used as a base for stuffing. For an extra kick, you might add diced jalapeños or a handful of shredded cheese.

Pumpkin bread deserves a mention, especially as the seasons turn cooler. This autumnal delight combines pureed pumpkin with warm spices like cinnamon, ginger, and cloves. The result is a fragrant loaf that evokes the essence of fall. Pumpkin bread can be enjoyed plain, with a simple glaze, or even a cream cheese frosting for a more decadent treat.

When it comes to quick breads and muffins, the choice of fat plays a significant role in the final product's texture and flavor. Butter, with its rich flavor, is a common choice, but oil can make for a moister bread. Applesauce or Greek yogurt can be used to replace some or all of the fat for a healthier option, though this might slightly alter the texture.

Sweeteners also vary. Granulated sugar is standard, but brown sugar adds a hint of molasses and extra moisture. Honey, maple syrup, or agave can provide a different kind of sweetness and depth of flavor. When using liquid sweeteners, it's crucial to adjust the amount of liquid in the recipe to maintain the proper consistency.

Add-ins are where quick breads and muffins truly shine. Nuts, seeds, dried fruits, chocolate chips, and spices can all be mixed in to create a unique flavor profile. For instance, a basic muffin recipe can be transformed into something extraordinary with the addition of lemon zest and poppy seeds, or perhaps by swirling in some Nutella before baking.

The baking process itself is straightforward but requires attention to detail. Preheating the oven is essential to ensure even cooking. Most quick breads bake at a moderate temperature, around 350°F (175°C), while muffins might bake at a slightly higher temperature to encourage a domed top. Using an oven thermometer can help maintain accuracy, as oven temperatures can often be unreliable.

Testing for doneness is another critical step. For quick breads, a toothpick inserted into the center should come out clean or with just a few crumbs clinging to it. Muffins are done when they spring back lightly when touched or a toothpick comes out clean. Overbaking can result in a dry texture, so it's better to check a few minutes early rather than risk dryness.

Cooling is often overlooked but plays a vital role in the final texture. Quick breads should cool in the pan for about 10 to 15 minutes before being transferred to a wire rack to cool completely. This allows the bread to set and makes it easier to slice without crumbling. Muffins, on the other hand, should cool in the pan for about 5 minutes before being removed to finish cooling on a wire rack. This brief cooling period helps them firm up slightly, making them less likely to fall apart when taken out of the tin.

Chapter 3

Lunchtime Favorites

Fresh and Flavorful Salads

Salads have evolved far beyond the basic lettuce and tomato combinations of the past. Today, they are vibrant, flavorful, and packed with an array of ingredients that cater to diverse palates and dietary needs. The key to creating a memorable salad lies in the balance of textures, flavors, and colors, transforming a simple dish into a culinary masterpiece.

One of the most critical elements of a great salad is the choice of greens. While iceberg lettuce has its place, there are many other varieties that offer more nutrition and flavor. Arugula, with its peppery bite, adds a dynamic contrast to sweeter ingredients. Spinach is another excellent choice, providing a mild flavor and a rich source of iron and vitamins. For a more robust foundation, consider kale or Swiss chard, both of which hold up well to hearty dressings and substantial toppings.

Once you've selected your greens, it's time to think about the other components. Vegetables are a natural choice, and the more colorful, the better. Red bell peppers, cherry tomatoes, and shredded carrots add a sweet crunch, while cucumbers and radishes bring a refreshing crispness. Don't be afraid to experiment with less common vegetables like roasted beets, grilled zucchini, or blanched asparagus. Each adds a unique flavor and texture that can elevate your salad.

Protein is an essential addition, especially if the salad is intended as a main course. Grilled chicken, shrimp, or steak are classic options that can be prepared in advance and served either warm or cold. For a vegetarian twist, consider adding hard-boiled eggs, chickpeas, or lentils. Cheese can also provide a protein boost and a rich, creamy texture; think crumbled feta, shredded Parmesan, or chunks of aged cheddar. Nuts and seeds, such as almonds, sunflower seeds, or pumpkin seeds, not only add protein but also a satisfying crunch.

Fruits can bring a surprising sweetness and juiciness to your salad. Fresh berries, such as strawberries, blueberries, or raspberries, are delightful in summer salads, while citrus segments like oranges or grapefruits add a burst of tangy flavor. In colder months, dried fruits like cranberries, apricots, or figs can add a chewy texture and concentrated sweetness.

Grains can transform a salad from a side dish into a hearty meal. Quinoa, farro, and bulgur are excellent choices that cook quickly and add a nutty, chewy texture. These grains can be mixed directly into the salad or served as a base with the other ingredients layered on top. Whole grains are not only filling but also provide essential nutrients and fiber.

Dressings are the final touch that brings all the elements of a salad together. A simple vinaigrette made with olive oil, vinegar, and a touch of mustard is a versatile option that pairs well with most salads. For a creamier dressing, consider using yogurt or avocado as a base. Fresh herbs like basil, cilantro, or dill can enhance the dressing's flavor and complement the salad ingredients. The key to a great dressing is balance: it should be flavorful but not overpowering, accentuating the salad's components rather than masking them.

Presentation is also important. A beautiful salad is a feast for the eyes as well as the palate. Arrange the ingredients thoughtfully, mixing colors and textures to create an appealing visual contrast. Use a large, shallow bowl to give the salad room to breathe and make it easier to toss the dressing evenly. Garnish with a sprinkle of fresh herbs, a pinch of sea salt, or a drizzle of good-quality olive oil to finish.

Consider the Greek salad, a classic example that showcases how simple ingredients can come together to create something extraordinary. Crisp cucumber, juicy tomatoes, and sharp red onion are combined with briny Kalamata olives and creamy feta cheese. A dressing of olive oil, lemon juice, oregano, and garlic ties everything together, creating a dish that is both refreshing and satisfying.

For a more exotic option, try a Thai-inspired salad. Shredded green papaya or mango forms the base, with carrots, bell peppers, and fresh herbs like mint and cilantro adding color and flavor. Grilled shrimp or chicken can provide protein, while a dressing of lime juice, fish sauce, chili, and sugar creates a perfect balance of sweet, sour, salty, and spicy.

A grain-based salad, such as a Mediterranean quinoa salad, can be both filling and nutritious. Cooked quinoa is mixed with cucumbers, tomatoes, red onion, and Kalamata olives. Fresh parsley and mint add a burst of freshness, while a lemon-tahini dressing provides a creamy, tangy finish. This salad can be made in advance and stored in the refrigerator, allowing the flavors to meld and intensify.

For a hearty winter salad, consider a combination of roasted vegetables and hearty greens. Roasted sweet potatoes, Brussels sprouts, and beets can be tossed with kale or arugula. A dressing of balsamic vinegar and Dijon mustard adds a tangy kick, while toasted walnuts or pecans provide crunch. Crumbled goat cheese or blue cheese can add a creamy texture and a touch of richness that contrasts beautifully with the earthy vegetables.

Hearty Sandwiches and Wraps

Hearty sandwiches and wraps are the epitome of convenience and culinary delight, offering endless possibilities for flavor, texture, and nutritional balance. Whether you're crafting a classic club sandwich, a vegetarian wrap, or a gourmet panini, the key to a memorable creation lies in the thoughtful combination of ingredients and attention to detail.

The foundation of any great sandwich or wrap starts with the bread or wrap itself. A sturdy, flavorful base sets the stage for the ingredients to shine. For sandwiches, consider options like ciabatta, sourdough, whole grain, or a crusty baguette. Each type of bread brings its own unique texture and taste, enhancing the overall experience. For wraps, options such as whole wheat, spinach, or tomato basil tortillas can add both flavor and color, making your creation visually appealing as well as delicious.

Next, think about the spread. A good spread not only adds moisture but also infuses the sandwich with additional flavor. Classic choices include mayonnaise, mustard, and butter, but don't hesitate to explore more adventurous options. Avocado spread, hummus, pesto, or even a tangy yogurt-based sauce can elevate a simple sandwich to gourmet status. The key is to match the spread to the other ingredients, ensuring a harmonious blend of flavors.

Protein is often the star of the sandwich or wrap, providing substance and satisfaction. Traditional choices like turkey, ham, roast beef, and chicken are always reliable, but there are plenty of other options to consider. Grilled vegetables, tofu, tempeh, or even a hearty bean spread can make for a delicious vegetarian alternative. For a touch of luxury, think about incorporating smoked salmon, prosciutto, or a marinated Portobello mushroom. The protein should be seasoned well and, if possible, prepared in advance to allow the flavors to develop.

Cheese is another essential component, adding both flavor and creaminess. From sharp cheddar and tangy Swiss to creamy brie and fresh mozzarella, the type of cheese you choose can significantly impact the overall taste. Think about how the cheese pairs with the other ingredients—sometimes a bold, aged cheese is perfect, while other times a mild, creamy cheese will complement without overpowering.

Vegetables add crunch, freshness, and color, making your sandwich or wrap not only more nutritious but also more enjoyable to eat. Crisp lettuce, juicy tomatoes, and thinly sliced cucumbers are classic choices, but don't be afraid to get creative. Roasted red peppers, pickled onions, shredded carrots, and even seasonal fruits like apple slices or figs can add unexpected flavors and textures. The goal is to balance the richness of the protein and cheese with the lightness and acidity of the vegetables.

Seasonings and condiments play a crucial role in tying all the elements together. A sprinkle of salt and pepper is a must, but additional spices and herbs can make a big difference. Think about adding fresh basil, cilantro, or arugula for a peppery bite, or a dash of smoked paprika, cumin, or chili flakes for warmth and depth. Condiments like pickles, olives, or a splash of vinegar can add a tangy contrast that brightens the overall flavor profile.

Layering is an art in itself. To avoid a soggy sandwich, start with a layer of greens or a sturdy vegetable like cucumber or bell pepper. Next, add your protein, then cheese, followed by any softer vegetables like tomatoes or avocado. Finally, top with another layer of greens or a thin spread to keep the bread from absorbing too much moisture. Wrapping tightly in parchment paper or foil can help maintain the structure, especially if you're packing the sandwich to go.

Consider the classic Reuben sandwich, a perfect example of how careful layering and balance of flavors can create a masterpiece. Start with rye bread, which provides a robust base. Spread each slice with Russian dressing, then layer on thin slices of corned beef, Swiss cheese, and sauerkraut. Grill the sandwich until the bread is golden and the cheese is melted, creating a perfect blend of savory, tangy, and creamy elements.

For a lighter option, a Mediterranean wrap can be both satisfying and refreshing. Use a whole wheat tortilla as your base, then spread a generous layer of hummus. Add slices of grilled chicken, cucumber, tomatoes, red onion, and a handful of fresh spinach. Drizzle with a bit of tzatziki sauce and sprinkle with feta cheese. Roll tightly and enjoy a wrap that bursts with fresh, vibrant flavors.

Another delightful choice is a vegetarian panini. Start with a ciabatta roll and spread both halves with pesto. Layer on grilled zucchini, roasted red peppers, fresh mozzarella, and a handful of arugula. Press the sandwich in a panini maker or grill it with a weight on top until the bread is crispy and the cheese is melted. This combination of Smokey, creamy, and peppery flavors is sure to satisfy even the most ardent meat lover.

For those who crave a bit of sweetness in their sandwiches, consider a turkey and cranberry wrap. Use a spinach tortilla and spread a thin layer of cream cheese on the tortilla. Add slices of roasted turkey, a handful of fresh spinach, and a generous spoonful of cranberry sauce. Roll it up tightly, ensuring that each bite delivers a perfect balance of savory turkey, creamy cheese, and sweet-tart cranberries. This wrap is perfect for using up holiday leftovers or simply enjoying a taste of Thanksgiving year-round.

Soups and Stews

Soups and stews are the soul-warming dishes that often evoke memories of home and comfort. They are versatile, nourishing, and perfect for any season. Whether you are a novice cook or an experienced chef, mastering the art of making soups and stews can elevate your culinary repertoire and provide endless meal options. The key to a successful soup or stew lies in the quality of ingredients, the layering of flavors, and the patient simmering that allows those flavors to meld together.

The base of any good soup or stew begins with the choice of liquid. Broths and stocks are the foundation, offering depth and richness. Homemade stocks—whether chicken, beef, vegetable, or seafood—are always preferred for their superior flavor. They can be made by simmering bones, vegetables, and aromatics for several hours, then straining the liquid. If you're short on time, high-quality store-bought broths can also work well. Just be mindful of the sodium content and opt for low-sodium versions when possible.

Aromatics like onions, garlic, carrots, and celery form the backbone of many soups and stews. These ingredients, often referred to as mirepoix in French cuisine, are typically sautéed in oil or butter at the beginning of the cooking process. This step, known as sweating, softens the vegetables and releases their flavors, creating a fragrant base for your dish. Building on this base, you can introduce additional vegetables, proteins, and seasonings.

Herbs and spices are crucial for adding complexity and depth to your soups and stews. Fresh herbs like thyme, rosemary, and parsley can provide bright, fresh notes, while dried herbs and spices like bay leaves, cumin, and paprika add warmth and earthiness. The timing of when you add these seasonings can affect the final flavor. For instance, adding fresh herbs towards the end preserves their vibrant flavor, while dried herbs can be added earlier to allow their flavors to infuse the broth.

Proteins, whether animal or plant-based, bring substance to soups and stews. Meats such as chicken, beef, pork, and lamb are classic choices, often browned first to develop a rich, caramelized flavor. This browning, known as the Maillard reaction, adds a depth of flavor that is integral to the dish. For a lighter option, seafood can be added towards the end of cooking to prevent overcooking. Plant-based proteins like beans, lentils, and tofu are excellent alternatives, offering both nutrition and heartiness.

Vegetables are the stars of many soups and stews, adding color, texture, and nutrients. Root vegetables like potatoes, carrots, and parsnips become tender and sweet when simmered. Leafy greens such as kale, spinach, and chard can be stirred in towards the end of cooking for a burst of color and freshness. Seasonal vegetables allow you to adapt your recipes throughout the year, taking advantage of the freshest produce available.

One of the joys of making soups and stews is the flexibility they offer. You can easily adapt recipes to suit your taste and dietary needs. For example, a classic beef stew can be transformed into a vegetarian delight by substituting mushrooms and beans for the meat. Similarly, a creamy potato leek soup can be made dairy-free by using coconut milk or a blend of cashews and water.

Consider the classic French onion soup, a perfect example of how simple ingredients can create a deeply flavorful dish. Thinly sliced onions are slowly caramelized until golden brown, then simmered in a rich beef broth with a splash of wine. The soup is topped with a slice of toasted baguette and a generous layer of melted Gruyère cheese. Each spoonful delivers a harmonious blend of sweet, savory, and cheesy goodness.

For a heartier option, think about making a traditional Irish stew. This dish typically features chunks of lamb or beef, potatoes, carrots, and onions, all simmered together in a flavorful broth. The key to a great Irish stew is the slow cooking process, which allows the meat to become tender and the flavors to meld together. A touch of fresh thyme and a splash of Guinness beer can add an extra depth of flavor.

If you're in the mood for something lighter, a classic chicken noodle soup can be incredibly comforting. Start by simmering chicken pieces with onions, carrots, and celery until the meat is tender. Remove the chicken to shred it, then return it to the pot with noodles and fresh herbs. A squeeze of lemon juice just before serving can brighten the flavors and add a refreshing twist.

For those who enjoy exploring international flavors, a Moroccan-inspired chickpea and lentil stew can be both exotic and satisfying. Aromatic spices like cumin, coriander, and cinnamon are sautéed with onions and garlic, then simmered with tomatoes, chickpeas, lentils, and vegetable broth. The result is a fragrant, hearty stew that's perfect for serving with a dollop of yogurt and a sprinkle of fresh cilantro.

Another delightful option is a Thai coconut soup, known as Tom Kha Gai. This soup combines the rich flavors of coconut milk, lemongrass, galangal, and kaffir lime leaves with tender pieces of chicken and mushrooms. The broth is both creamy and tangy, thanks to the addition of lime juice and fish sauce. Garnish with fresh cilantro and thinly sliced red chili for a burst of color and heat. Each spoonful offers a delicate balance of sweet, sour, salty, and spicy flavors that are characteristic of Thai cuisine.

Grain Bowls and Power Lunches

Grain bowls and power lunches have emerged as popular choices for those seeking nutritious, convenient meals that pack a punch of energy and flavor. These meals are not only visually appealing but also versatile, allowing for endless customization based on personal preferences and dietary needs. By combining a variety of grains, proteins, vegetables, and dressings, you can create balanced meals that nourish the body and delight the palate.

The foundation of a great grain bowl starts with the grains themselves. Options like quinoa, farro, brown rice, barley, and bulgur offer different textures and flavors, each bringing its own nutritional benefits. Quinoa, for example, is a complete protein, making it an excellent choice for vegetarians and vegans. Farro, an ancient grain, is rich in fiber and has a pleasantly chewy texture. Brown rice is a familiar staple that provides a mild, nutty flavor and pairs well with almost any ingredient.

Cooking grains properly is crucial to achieving the right texture. It's essential to rinse grains like quinoa and farro before cooking to remove any bitterness. The water-to-grain ratio, cooking time, and whether to cover the pot can vary between grains. Quinoa typically requires one part grain to two parts water and cooks in about 15 minutes, while farro might need a bit more water and up to 30 minutes of simmering. Experimenting with different grains can help you find your favorites and understand how to cook them to perfection.

Once you've selected and cooked your grains, the next step is to choose the proteins. Protein sources can range from animal-based options like grilled chicken, beef, shrimp, or boiled eggs to plant-based choices such as chickpeas, lentils, tofu, or tempeh. Grilled chicken breast, seasoned with herbs and spices, adds a lean and flavorful protein to your bowl. For a plant-based option, consider roasting chickpeas with olive oil, garlic powder, and smoked paprika until crispy. These add a delightful crunch and a burst of flavor.

Vegetables are the heart of any grain bowl, providing essential vitamins, minerals, and fiber. The variety of vegetables you can use is virtually endless. Roasted vegetables like sweet potatoes, bell peppers, zucchini, and Brussels sprouts add a caramelized sweetness and depth of flavor. Fresh vegetables such as spinach, kale, arugula, and cabbage bring a crisp, refreshing contrast. You can also include fermented vegetables like kimchi or sauerkraut for a tangy, probiotic-rich addition.

Balancing textures is key to a satisfying grain bowl. Combining crunchy elements like nuts, seeds, and fresh vegetables with softer components like roasted vegetables and cooked grains creates a more interesting and enjoyable eating experience. For example, sprinkle toasted pumpkin seeds or slivered almonds over your bowl for added crunch. Incorporating creamy elements, such as avocado slices or a dollop of hummus, can also enhance the overall texture and flavor profile.

Dressings and sauces tie all the components of a grain bowl together, infusing the dish with additional flavors. A simple vinaigrette made with olive oil, lemon juice, Dijon mustard, and honey can brighten up your bowl and add a zesty kick. For a more robust flavor, try a tahini-based dressing with garlic, lemon juice, and a touch of maple syrup. Peanut sauce, made from peanut butter, soy sauce, ginger, and lime juice, can bring an Asian-inspired twist. Experimenting with different dressings allows you to tailor the flavor profile to your liking.

Power lunches, on the other hand, are designed to provide sustained energy and focus throughout the afternoon. These meals should be balanced, combining lean proteins, complex carbohydrates, healthy fats, and plenty of fiber. They can take various forms, from salads and wraps to more traditional plated meals, but the principles of balance and nutrition remain the same.

A classic example of a power lunch is the Mediterranean-inspired salad. Start with a base of mixed greens, such as spinach, arugula, and romaine lettuce. Add cherry tomatoes, cucumbers, red onions, and Kalamata olives for a burst of color and flavor. Incorporate a protein source like grilled chicken, tuna, or chickpeas. Top with crumbled feta cheese and a handful of quinoa for extra texture and nutrition. Dress the salad with a simple olive oil and lemon dressing, seasoned with oregano, salt, and pepper. This salad is not only delicious but also packed with nutrients that support sustained energy.

Wraps are another excellent option for power lunches, offering a convenient and portable meal. Whole-grain tortillas or wraps provide a good source of complex carbohydrates. Fill them with a variety of ingredients, such as grilled vegetables, lean meats, and beans. A southwestern-inspired wrap might include grilled chicken, black beans, corn, avocado, and a sprinkle of cheddar cheese, all wrapped in a whole-wheat tortilla. A drizzle of lime-cilantro dressing can add a fresh, tangy flavor.

For those who prefer a more traditional plated lunch, a balanced approach can still be achieved. Start with a lean protein, such as salmon or tofu, paired with a complex carbohydrate like quinoa, brown rice, or sweet potatoes. Add a generous portion of vegetables, either steamed, roasted, or fresh, to make up at least half of your plate. For instance, a plate featuring grilled salmon, quinoa, and a medley of roasted vegetables such as carrots, broccoli, and bell peppers offers a well-rounded meal that is both satisfying and nutritious. A squeeze of lemon over the salmon and a drizzle of olive oil on the veggies can enhance the flavors and provide healthy fats.

Light and Easy Lunch Ideas

Lunchtime often becomes a hurried affair, squeezed between meetings, errands, and the demands of daily life. Yet, a thoughtfully prepared lunch can transform your midday meal into a moment of rejuvenation and enjoyment. Light and easy lunch ideas are not just about convenience; they are about crafting meals that are nutritious, delicious, and simple to prepare. This chapter delves into a variety of strategies and recipes to ensure your lunches are both satisfying and effortless.

Salads are a quintessential light lunch option, offering endless possibilities for flavor combinations and nutritional benefits. One of the simplest ways to elevate a salad is by focusing on fresh, seasonal ingredients. Imagine a summer salad with juicy cherry tomatoes, crisp cucumbers, sweet corn kernels, and tangy feta cheese, all tossed in a light lemon vinaigrette. The freshness of the produce shines through, and the contrasting flavors and textures create a delightful eating experience. To make your salads more substantial, consider adding a protein source such as grilled chicken, chickpeas, or hard-boiled eggs.

Wraps and sandwiches are another excellent choice for a light lunch. They are portable, easy to assemble, and can be tailored to suit any taste preference. A Mediterranean-inspired wrap, for example, could include hummus, roasted red peppers, cucumbers, olives, and spinach, all wrapped in a whole-grain tortilla. The hummus provides a creamy base, while the vegetables add crunch and flavor. For those who prefer a heartier sandwich, layering ingredients like turkey, avocado, sprouts, and a smear of mustard on whole-grain bread can offer a satisfying and nutritious option.

Soups, particularly those that are broth-based, can be both light and filling. They are ideal for preparing in large batches and reheating throughout the week. A vegetable minestrone, brimming with carrots, celery, zucchini, tomatoes, and beans, provides a comforting and nutrient-dense lunch. Adding a handful of whole-grain pasta or quinoa can make the soup more substantial without weighing you down. Gazpacho, a chilled tomato-based soup, is perfect for hot days and can be made ahead, allowing the flavors to meld beautifully.

For those who prefer something a bit different, grain bowls offer a versatile and satisfying lunch option. Start with a base of cooked grains like quinoa, bulgur, or farro, and top with a variety of vegetables, proteins, and dressings. A particularly delightful combination includes quinoa, roasted sweet potatoes, black beans, avocado, and a drizzle of lime-cilantro dressing. The grains provide a wholesome foundation, while the vegetables and beans add color, texture, and flavor. Grain bowls are also an excellent way to use up leftovers, as nearly any cooked vegetable or protein can be incorporated.

Egg-based dishes such as frittatas and omelets can be surprisingly light and are an excellent way to incorporate more vegetables into your diet. A frittata made with spinach, cherry tomatoes, and feta cheese is both flavorful and easy to prepare. It can be cooked in advance and enjoyed cold or at room temperature, making it a convenient option for busy days. Similarly, an omelet filled with mushrooms, bell peppers, and a sprinkle of cheese can be whipped up in minutes and provides a balanced meal that is high in protein.

Incorporating fruits and nuts into your lunch can add a refreshing twist and a boost of energy. A simple fruit and nut salad, combining mixed greens, sliced apples, walnuts, and a light vinaigrette, offers a balance of sweet, savory, and crunchy elements. Adding a bit of goat cheese or blue cheese can elevate the flavors and make the salad more satisfying. This type of meal is not only light but also rich in antioxidants, vitamins, and healthy fats.

Meal prepping can significantly simplify the process of making light and easy lunches. By dedicating some time at the beginning of the week to prepare ingredients, you can ensure that nutritious options are always within reach. Cook a batch of grains, roast a variety of vegetables, and prepare a few proteins like grilled chicken or tofu. Store these components separately in the refrigerator, and mix and match them to create different lunches throughout the week. This approach saves time and reduces the temptation to opt for less healthy convenience foods.

Another practical tip for creating light lunches is to embrace simplicity. Sometimes, the most delicious meals are the simplest ones. A plate of sliced tomatoes, fresh mozzarella, and basil drizzled with olive oil and balsamic vinegar is a classic example.

This Caprese salad is not only quick to assemble but also highlights the natural flavors of the ingredients. Similarly, a bowl of mixed berries topped with a dollop of Greek yogurt and a sprinkle of granola makes for a refreshing and light lunch that satisfies sweet cravings.

Incorporating a variety of textures in your meals can make light lunches more enjoyable. Think about crunchy vegetables, creamy dressings, and chewy grains. A salad with mixed greens, shredded carrots, edamame, crispy wonton strips, and a sesame-ginger dressing offers a delightful mix of textures that keeps each bite interesting. Adding a handful of toasted nuts or seeds can further enhance the textural contrast, adding both crunch and flavor. This variety in texture not only makes the meal more enjoyable but also helps in making you feel more satisfied.

Chapter 4

Dinners to Impress

One-Pot and Skillet Meals

The allure of one-pot and skillet meals lies in their simplicity and the promise of minimal cleanup. These meals are designed to maximize flavor while streamlining the cooking process, making them an ideal choice for busy households, novice cooks, and anyone looking to spend less time in the kitchen.

Imagine coming home after a long day, tired and hungry, the last thing you want is a complicated recipe with a mountain of dishes to wash. Enter the one-pot meal, where everything cooks together in harmony. Picture a hearty chicken and rice dish infused with aromatic herbs and spices. Start by searing chicken thighs in a large pot, creating a golden crust. Remove the chicken, then in the same pot, sauté diced onions, garlic, and bell peppers until they soften and release their fragrance. Add rice, chicken broth, and a mix of seasonings like paprika, thyme, and bay leaves. Nestle the chicken back into the pot, cover, and let it simmer until the rice is tender and the chicken is cooked through. The result? A comforting, flavorful meal with minimal effort and maximum satisfaction.

Skillet meals offer a similar convenience, often with the added benefit of a quicker cooking time. Consider a classic beef stir-fry. Thinly sliced beef is quickly browned in a hot skillet, then set aside while a medley of colorful vegetables like broccoli, bell peppers, and snap peas are stir-fried until just tender. A simple sauce of soy sauce, ginger, garlic, and a touch of honey is poured into the skillet, the beef is added back in, and everything is tossed together until well-coated and heated through. Serve over a bed of steamed rice or noodles, and you have a balanced, nutritious meal ready in under 30 minutes.

The versatility of one-pot and skillet meals means they can be adapted to any cuisine or dietary preference. For a vegetarian option, consider a one-pot pasta primavera. In a large pot, sauté garlic and onions in olive oil until translucent. Add vegetable broth, diced tomatoes, and your choice of mixed vegetables such as zucchini, bell peppers, and cherry tomatoes. Bring to a boil, then add pasta directly into the pot, allowing it to cook and absorb the flavors of the broth and vegetables. Finish with a handful of fresh basil, a sprinkle of Parmesan cheese, and a drizzle of olive oil. The pasta is perfectly al dente, and the vegetables retain their vibrant color and crispness.

For a seafood twist, a skillet shrimp and asparagus dish is both light and flavorful. Start by heating a bit of olive oil in a large skillet, then add minced garlic and cook until fragrant. Toss in fresh shrimp, seasoned with salt, pepper, and a pinch of red pepper flakes. Cook until the shrimp turn pink, then remove them from the skillet. In the same skillet, add trimmed asparagus spears and a splash of chicken broth or white wine. Cook until the asparagus is tender-crisp, then return the shrimp to the skillet, tossing everything together with a squeeze of fresh lemon juice and a sprinkle of parsley.

One-pot and skillet meals are also perfect for incorporating whole grains into your diet. A one-pot quinoa and black bean chili is a robust, protein-packed option. In a large pot, sauté onions, garlic, and bell peppers until softened. Add quinoa, black beans, diced tomatoes, corn, and a blend of spices such as cumin, chili powder, and oregano. Pour in vegetable broth, bring to a boil, then reduce the heat and simmer until the quinoa is cooked and the flavors meld together. Serve with a dollop of Greek yogurt, a sprinkle of cheese, and a handful of fresh cilantro.

For breakfast or brunch, a skillet frittata is a versatile dish that can be customized with your favorite ingredients. Begin by whisking together eggs, a splash of milk, salt, and pepper. Heat a bit of butter or oil in a skillet, then add diced vegetables like onions, bell peppers, and spinach. Cook until the vegetables are tender, then pour the egg mixture over them. Sprinkle with cheese and transfer the skillet to the oven to bake until the eggs are set and the top is golden brown. Slice into wedges and serve with a side of toast or a simple green salad.

One of the key benefits of one-pot and skillet meals is the layering of flavors. When ingredients are cooked together in the same vessel, they have the opportunity to infuse and enhance each other, creating a depth of flavor that can be hard to achieve with separate cooking methods. This technique is particularly effective in dishes like a one-pot creamy mushroom risotto. Start by sautéing shallots and garlic in butter until softened. Add Arborio rice, stirring to coat each grain with the buttery mixture. Gradually add warm broth, one ladle at a time, stirring continuously until the liquid is absorbed and the rice becomes creamy and tender. Stir in sautéed mushrooms, a splash of white wine, and a generous handful of grated Parmesan cheese. The result is a rich, velvety risotto with layers of umami flavor from the mushrooms and cheese and a subtle hint of wine that elevates the dish.

Pasta and Rice Dishes

Pasta and rice dishes, staples in many households worldwide, offer an endless variety of flavors and textures that can please any palate. These versatile ingredients serve as the foundation for numerous culinary traditions, from the comforting classics of Italian cuisine to the spicy, robust dishes of Asian cultures. Understanding how to prepare and enhance these dishes can elevate your cooking, turning simple ingredients into memorable meals.

Let's begin with pasta. This humble ingredient, made from durum wheat and water, comes in countless shapes and sizes, each suited to different types of sauces and preparation methods. Spaghetti, fettuccine, penne, and farfalle are just a few examples of the diversity that pasta offers. The key to mastering pasta dishes lies in understanding the balance between pasta and sauce—how the shape and texture of the pasta can complement or contrast with the sauce to create a harmonious dish.

Cooking pasta to perfection starts with the boiling process. Use a large pot of salted water, ensuring there is ample space for the pasta to move as it cooks. The water should taste like the sea—this is essential for seasoning the pasta from within. Once the water reaches a rolling boil, add the pasta and stir occasionally to prevent sticking. Cooking times vary depending on the type and thickness of the pasta, so always refer to the package instructions and taste for doneness. Al dente, meaning "to the tooth," is the ideal texture: firm yet tender.

One classic pasta dish that epitomizes simplicity and flavor is Spaghetti Aglio e Olio. This dish, originating from Naples, consists of spaghetti, garlic, olive oil, red pepper flakes, and parsley. The beauty of Spaghetti Agile e Olio lies in its minimalist approach, allowing each ingredient to shine. Start by heating olive oil in a pan, adding thinly sliced garlic and red pepper flakes to infuse the oil with their flavors. Cook the garlic until it turns golden but not burnt, as overcooked garlic can taste bitter. Toss the cooked spaghetti in the flavored oil and garlic mixture, adding a splash of pasta water to create a silky emulsion that coats the pasta. Finish with chopped parsley and a sprinkle of sea salt.

For a heartier pasta experience, consider a Bolognese sauce. This rich, meaty sauce is traditionally served with tagliatelle or pappardelle, wide noodles that can hold the robust sauce. Bolognese starts with a soffritto—a mixture of finely chopped onions, carrots, and celery sautéed in olive oil. Add ground meat (typically a mix of beef and pork) and cook until browned. Deglaze the pan with red wine, allowing it to reduce before adding tomatoes, milk, and a bouquet of herbs. Let the sauce simmer slowly for several hours, developing deep, complex flavors. The result is a thick, savory sauce that clings to the pasta, offering a satisfying bite with each forkful.

Rice dishes offer a different set of challenges and rewards. Rice, like pasta, comes in many varieties, each with its unique characteristics. Basmati, jasmine, Arborio, and sushi rice are just a few examples, each suited to specific types of dishes. The key to a successful rice dish lies in selecting the right type of rice and mastering the cooking technique.

One of the most beloved rice dishes globally is the Spanish paella. Originating from the Valencia region, paella is a vibrant, communal dish cooked in a wide, shallow pan. The essential ingredients include short-grain rice, saffron, and a mix of proteins such as chicken, rabbit, and seafood. The preparation begins with a sofrito, a base of grated tomatoes, onions, and garlic cooked in olive oil. Once the sofrito is ready, add the rice, stirring to coat each grain with the flavorful base. Pour in a mixture of stock and saffron, bringing it to a boil before reducing the heat. Arrange the proteins and vegetables atop the rice, allowing the dish to simmer without stirring, creating a crispy layer of socarrat at the bottom. The result is a colorful, aromatic dish that encapsulates the essence of Spanish cuisine.

In Asian cuisine, rice often takes center stage, serving as the foundation for various dishes. One such dish is the Thai classic, Pad Kra Pao. This spicy stir-fry features ground meat, typically pork or chicken, cooked with garlic, chili, and holy basil. The dish is served over jasmine rice and topped with a fried egg. The key to Pad Kra Pao is the balance of flavors—spicy, savory, and slightly sweet. Start by pounding garlic and chilies into a paste, then stir-fry the mixture in hot oil. Add the ground meat, cooking until browned, and season with fish sauce, soy sauce, and a touch of sugar. Toss in the holy basil at the end, allowing it to wilt and release its fragrant aroma. Serve immediately over steamed jasmine rice, with the runny yolk of the fried egg adding a rich, velvety texture to the dish. Risotto, an Italian classic, showcases how rice can transform into a creamy, luxurious dish. Arborio or Carniola rice, known for its high starch content, is essential for achieving the desired texture. Begin by sautéing finely chopped onions in butter until translucent. Add the rice, stirring to coat each grain with the butter and toasting lightly. This step is crucial as it helps the rice absorb the liquid evenly. Slowly add warm broth, one ladle at a time, allowing the rice to absorb the liquid before adding more. Stir continuously, which helps release the rice's starch, creating a creamy consistency. The final touch is to stir in grated Parmesan cheese and a knob of butter, enriching the risotto with a velvety finish. Risotto can be customized with a variety of ingredients, such as mushrooms, seafood, or saffron, each bringing unique flavors to the dish.

Savory Meat and Poultry Entrees

Savory meat and poultry entrées are the heart of many memorable meals, providing rich, satisfying flavors and a depth of culinary possibilities. From the robust, slow-cooked stews of European traditions to the quick, fiery stir-fries of Asian cuisines, these dishes highlight the versatility and appeal of meat and poultry. Understanding the basics of selecting, preparing, and cooking these proteins can transform your cooking from mundane to extraordinary.

Selecting the right cut of meat or poultry is the first step toward a successful dish. Each type of meat has various cuts, each suited to different cooking methods. For instance, beef offers a range of options from tenderloin, perfect for quick grilling, to brisket, ideal for slow braising. Similarly, chicken can be purchased whole or in parts, such as breasts, thighs, and wings, each offering distinct textures and flavors. Freshness is key; always look for bright, firm flesh and avoid any with off smells or discoloration.

Marinating is a powerful technique to infuse meat and poultry with flavor and tenderize tougher cuts. A good marinade typically includes an acid (such as vinegar or citrus juice), oil, and various seasonings. The acid helps break down muscle fibers, making the meat more tender, while the oil and seasonings impart flavor. For example, a classic marinade for beef might include red wine, garlic, rosemary, and olive oil, while a more exotic blend for chicken could feature yogurt, lemon juice, cumin, and coriander. Allow the meat to marinate for at least a few hours, or overnight for more intense flavor.

One of the most renowned beef dishes is the French classic, Beef Bourguignon. This dish transforms a tough cut of beef, such as chuck, into a tender, flavorful masterpiece through slow braising. Start by browning chunks of beef in a heavy pot to develop a deep, caramelized crust. Remove the beef and sauté onions, carrots, and garlic in the same pot, scraping up the browned bits from the bottom. Return the beef to the pot and add red wine, beef broth, tomato paste, and a bouquet garni of fresh herbs. Simmer the mixture slowly until the beef is fork-tender and the sauce has thickened into a rich, velvety consistency. Serve with mashed potatoes or crusty bread to soak up the delicious sauce.

Chicken, a staple in many kitchens, offers endless possibilities for creativity. Roast chicken is a timeless favorite, delivering crispy skin and juicy, flavorful meat. Begin by choosing a whole chicken, preferably organic for the best flavor. Pat the chicken dry and season it generously with salt and pepper, both inside and out. Stuff the cavity with aromatics like lemon halves, garlic cloves, and fresh herbs such as thyme and rosemary. Rub the skin with olive oil or melted butter to help it crisp up during roasting. Place the chicken in a preheated oven and roast until the skin is golden brown and the meat reaches an internal temperature of 165°F. Let the chicken rest before carving to allow the juices to redistribute, ensuring moist, tender meat.

For a quicker option, consider a stir-fry. This method, popular in many Asian cuisines, is perfect for busy weeknights. The key to a successful stir-fry is high heat and fast cooking. Cut your meat or poultry into thin, uniform slices to ensure even cooking. Heat a wok or large skillet until very hot, then add a high-smoke-point oil, such as peanut or canola oil. Add the meat or poultry and stir-fry until browned and cooked through. Remove it from the pan and stir-fry vegetables like bell peppers, broccoli, and snap peas until tender-crisp. Return the meat to the pan, add a flavorful sauce made from soy sauce, garlic, ginger, and a touch of sugar, and toss everything together until well coated. Serve immediately over steamed rice or noodles.

Pork, often underappreciated, can be incredibly flavorful and versatile. One standout dish is pork tenderloin, which is lean, tender, and quick-cooking. To prepare, season the tenderloin with a blend of spices such as paprika, garlic powder, and cumin. Sear the meat in a hot skillet until browned on all sides, then finish cooking in the oven until it reaches an internal temperature of 145°F. Let the pork rest before slicing to retain its juices. Serve with a simple pan sauce made from the drippings, deglazed with apple cider and finished with a touch of mustard and honey for a sweet and tangy complement.

Lamb, with its distinct, rich flavor, is a favorite in many cultures. A classic preparation is the Greek dish, lamb souvlaki. Marinate cubes of lamb in a mixture of olive oil, lemon juice, garlic, oregano, and black pepper for several hours. Thread the lamb onto skewers and grill over high heat until charred on the outside and tender on the inside. Serve the souvlaki with warm pita bread, a tangy tzatziki sauce made from yogurt, cucumber, and dill, and a fresh Greek salad featuring tomatoes, cucumbers, olives, and feta cheese. The combination of the smoky, flavorful lamb with the cool, creamy tzatziki and crisp salad creates a harmonious and satisfying meal.

Seafood Sensations

Seafood sensations tantalize the palate with their delicate flavors and varied textures, offering a bounty of culinary delights from the world's oceans, rivers, and lakes. The key to mastering seafood dishes lies in selecting the freshest ingredients, understanding the unique characteristics of each type of seafood, and employing cooking techniques that highlight their natural flavors while preserving their nutritional benefits.

Freshness is paramount when it comes to seafood. Whether purchasing fish, shellfish, or mollusks, always look for signs of freshness. Fish should have bright, clear eyes, shiny skin, and a clean, ocean-like smell. Shellfish, like clams and mussels, should have tightly closed shells or close when tapped lightly. For shrimp and other crustaceans, the shells should be firm, and the flesh should be translucent and moist. Once you've selected your seafood, it's important to store it properly. Keep it cold, ideally on ice, and cook it within a day or two to ensure the best quality and flavor.

One of the most popular and versatile seafood options is salmon. Rich in omega-3 fatty acids, salmon is not only delicious but also packed with health benefits. There are numerous ways to prepare salmon, but one of the simplest and most flavorful methods is grilling. Start by marinating the salmon in a mixture of olive oil, lemon juice, garlic, and fresh herbs like dill or parsley. Preheat your grill to medium-high heat and oil the grates to prevent sticking. Grill the salmon skin-side down for about six to eight minutes per side, depending on thickness, until the flesh is opaque and flakes easily with a fork. Serve with a side of grilled vegetables or a fresh salad for a light, healthy meal.

Shrimp, another favorite, cooks quickly and is incredibly versatile. A classic shrimp dish is shrimp scampi, which showcases the natural sweetness of shrimp in a rich, garlicky butter sauce. Begin by sautéing minced garlic in a generous amount of butter and olive oil until fragrant. Add peeled and deveined shrimp, cooking until they just turn pink and opaque. Deglaze the pan with white wine and lemon juice, then toss with cooked linguine and a sprinkle of fresh parsley. The result is a luxurious, yet simple dish that's perfect for a quick weeknight dinner or an elegant dinner party.

For a taste of the Mediterranean, consider preparing a seafood paella. This traditional Spanish dish combines a variety of seafood with saffron-infused rice, vegetables, and aromatic spices. Start by heating olive oil in a large, shallow pan and sautéing onions, garlic, and bell peppers until softened. Add rice and stir to coat with the oil and vegetables, then pour in a mixture of chicken broth and saffron threads. As the rice begins to cook, arrange an assortment of seafood on top, such as mussels, clams, shrimp, and squid. Cover the pan and simmer until the rice is tender and the seafood is cooked through. Garnish with fresh lemon wedges and chopped parsley before serving.

Scallops, with their sweet, delicate flavor and firm texture, are a true delicacy. Perfectly seared scallops are a simple yet impressive dish that can be mastered with a few key techniques. Pat the scallops dry with paper towels to ensure a good sear and season with salt and pepper. Heat a mixture of butter and oil in a hot skillet until shimmering, then add the scallops, making sure not to overcrowd the pan. Sear for about two minutes per side until a golden crust forms and the scallops are just opaque in the center. Serve with a drizzle of lemon butter sauce and a side of risotto or sautéed greens for a refined, restaurant-quality meal.

For those who enjoy the briny flavor of shellfish, a classic clam chowder is a must-try. This creamy, hearty soup is a staple of New England cuisine and is perfect for a cozy meal. Begin by cooking diced bacon in a large pot until crispy, then remove and set aside. In the same pot, sauté onions and celery in the rendered bacon fat until softened. Add diced potatoes, clam juice, and fresh or canned clams, then simmer until the potatoes are tender. Stir in heavy cream and season with salt, pepper, and a splash of Worcestershire sauce. Garnish with the reserved bacon and fresh parsley, and serve with oyster crackers or crusty bread.

Octopus, often perceived as challenging to prepare, can be incredibly tender and flavorful when cooked properly. One popular method is to braise the octopus slowly until tender, then finish it on the grill for a smoky char. Start by simmering the octopus in a pot of water with aromatics like bay leaves, peppercorns, and lemon slices for about an hour until tender. Remove the octopus, pat dry, and cut into manageable pieces. Brush with olive oil and grill over high heat for a few minutes until charred and crispy. Serve with a drizzle of lemon and olive oil, and a side of roasted potatoes or a simple salad.

For those looking to explore more exotic seafood options, squid is an excellent choice. Known for its firm texture and mild flavor, squid can be prepared in a variety of ways, from frying to grilling. One beloved dish is calamari, which features breaded and fried squid rings. To prepare, slice the cleaned squid into rings, then soak in buttermilk to tenderize. Dredge the rings in a mixture of flour, cornmeal, salt, and pepper, then fry in hot oil until golden and crispy. Serve with lemon wedges and a dipping sauce, such as marinara or aioli, for a delightful appetizer or snack.

Vegetarian and Vegan Mains

In the vibrant world of vegetarian and vegan cuisine, the possibilities for creating satisfying, flavorful main dishes are endless. Embracing plant-based eating means diving into a rich tapestry of ingredients and techniques that can transform humble vegetables, legumes, grains, and fruits into culinary masterpieces. The key to successful vegetarian and vegan cooking lies in understanding how to build complex flavors, textures, and nutrients into every dish, ensuring that each meal is not only delicious but also balanced and nourishing.

One of the cornerstones of vegetarian and vegan mains is the use of legumes, which provide a substantial source of protein and fiber. Lentils, chickpeas, black beans, and more can be the foundation of many hearty dishes. Take, for example, a classic lentil stew. Start by sautéing onions, garlic, carrots, and celery in a large pot until softened. Add in dried lentils, vegetable broth, diced tomatoes, and a blend of spices like cumin, paprika, and thyme. Simmer until the lentils are tender and the flavors meld together. The result is a comforting, protein-packed stew that pairs perfectly with crusty bread or a side salad.

Chickpeas, another versatile legume, shine in dishes like chickpea curry. Begin by heating oil in a pan and adding mustard seeds until they start to pop. Then, sauté onions, garlic, and ginger until fragrant. Stir in curry powder, turmeric, and ground coriander, followed by canned chickpeas and coconut milk. Simmer until the sauce thickens and the chickpeas are infused with the rich, aromatic flavors. Serve over steamed basmati rice or with warm naan bread for a meal that's both satisfying and packed with plant-based protein.

Grains also play a crucial role in vegetarian and vegan mains, offering a hearty base that can be dressed up in countless ways. Quinoa, for instance, is a complete protein and works wonderfully in dishes like stuffed bell peppers. Cook quinoa according to package instructions and mix with black beans, corn, diced tomatoes, and spices such as cumin and chili powder. Hollow out bell peppers and fill them with the quinoa mixture, then bake until the peppers are tender. Top with fresh cilantro and a squeeze of lime for a vibrant, nutrient-dense meal.

Another grain that lends itself well to plant-based cooking is farro. With its chewy texture and nutty flavor, farro adds depth to dishes like farro risotto. Unlike traditional risotto, which relies on Arborio rice and a slow, careful stirring process, farro risotto is more forgiving and can be prepared with less fuss. Sauté onions and garlic in olive oil, then add farro and toast it briefly before adding vegetable broth, one ladle at a time, until the farro is tender. Stir in seasonal vegetables like mushrooms, asparagus, or butternut squash, along with a splash of white wine and a handful of fresh herbs. The result is a creamy, savory dish that's both comforting and elegant.

Vegetables themselves can be the star of the show in vegetarian and vegan mains. Take, for instance, the humble cauliflower, which can be transformed into a stunning main dish with the right preparation. A whole roasted cauliflower, marinated in a blend of olive oil, lemon juice, garlic, and spices like turmeric and smoked paprika, becomes a centerpiece-worthy dish. Roast until the cauliflower is tender and golden brown, then serve with a tahini sauce and a sprinkle of fresh parsley for a meal that's as visually impressive as it is delicious.

Eggplant is another vegetable that can take center stage in plant-based cooking. For a Mediterranean-inspired dish, try making stuffed eggplant. Halve the eggplants and scoop out the flesh, then sauté the chopped eggplant with onions, tomatoes, garlic, and a mix of spices like cumin, coriander, and cinnamon. Fill the eggplant shells with the mixture and bake until tender. Top with a drizzle of olive oil and a sprinkle of pine nuts for added texture and flavor.

For those who enjoy more substantial, protein-rich vegetables, mushrooms are a fantastic option. Portobello mushrooms, in particular, are meaty and satisfying. Try grilling marinated Portobello mushroom caps as a hearty alternative to burgers. Marinate the mushrooms in a mixture of balsamic vinegar, soy sauce, garlic, and olive oil, then grill until tender and slightly charred. Serve on a toasted bun with all your favorite burger toppings, or slice and add to a grain bowl for a filling, nutritious meal.

Tofu and tempeh are staples in vegan cooking, providing a versatile canvas for a variety of flavors. Tofu, with its mild taste and ability to absorb marinades, can be used in countless dishes. For a quick and flavorful main, try tofu stir-fry. Press the tofu to remove excess moisture, then cut into cubes and marinate in soy sauce, ginger, and garlic. Stir-fry with a mix of colorful vegetables like bell peppers, broccoli, and snap peas, and finish with a splash of sesame oil and a sprinkle of sesame seeds.

Tempeh, with its firmer texture and nutty flavor, is another excellent protein source that adds depth to plant-based dishes. A tempeh stir-fry can be a delightful variation. Slice the tempeh into thin strips and marinate in a mixture of tamari, maple syrup, garlic, and ginger. Stir-fry over high heat until golden brown and crispy, then add vegetables like bok choy, shiitake mushrooms, and carrots. Finish with a splash of rice vinegar and a handful of fresh herbs, such as cilantro or basil, for a dish that's full of umami and satisfying textures.

Chapter 5

Sides and Small Plates

Roasted and Grilled Vegetables

Roasted and grilled vegetables are not just side dishes; they can be the centerpiece of a meal, bursting with flavors, textures, and colors that are both visually appealing and incredibly satisfying. The magic of roasting and grilling lies in the transformation that occurs when vegetables are exposed to high heat. The natural sugars caramelize, creating deeper, more complex flavors, while the exterior becomes beautifully charred and crisp.

Roasting vegetables is a straightforward technique that yields consistently delicious results. Begin with a selection of your favorite vegetables. Root vegetables like carrots, parsnips, and sweet potatoes develop a rich sweetness when roasted, while cruciferous vegetables such as broccoli, cauliflower, and Brussels sprouts take on a nutty flavor and crispy edges. Even more delicate vegetables like zucchini, bell peppers, and onions can be elevated through roasting.

Start by preheating your oven to 425°F (220°C). This high temperature ensures that the vegetables will cook quickly and develop a nice caramelized exterior. Cut the vegetables into uniform pieces to ensure even cooking. Toss them in a generous amount of olive oil, which helps in achieving that coveted crispy texture and enhances the flavor. Season with salt, pepper, and any other herbs or spices you enjoy. Rosemary, thyme, and garlic are classic choices, but don't be afraid to experiment with cumin, smoked paprika, or curry powder for a different twist.

Spread the vegetables in a single layer on a baking sheet. Overcrowding the pan can lead to steaming rather than roasting, so use two baking sheets if necessary. Roast in the preheated oven, stirring once or twice during cooking to ensure even browning. Most vegetables will be perfectly roasted in 20-30 minutes, but keep an eye on them, as cooking times can vary based on the size and type of vegetable.

Grilling offers another dimension to vegetable cooking, adding a smoky flavor that is particularly appealing. Almost any vegetable can be grilled, but some of the best include bell peppers, zucchini, eggplant, asparagus, and corn. Start by preheating your grill to medium-high heat. As with roasting, cutting the vegetables to a uniform size is crucial for even cooking. Larger vegetables like bell peppers and eggplant can be sliced into thick strips or rounds, while smaller vegetables like asparagus can be left whole.

Brush the vegetables with olive oil and season with salt and pepper. You can also marinate them beforehand for added flavor. A simple marinade of balsamic vinegar, garlic, and fresh herbs can work wonders. Place the vegetables directly on the grill grates or use a grill basket for smaller pieces. Grill the vegetables, turning occasionally, until they are tender and charred in spots. This typically takes about 5-10 minutes per side, depending on the vegetable and thickness.

One of the joys of roasting and grilling vegetables is their versatility. A platter of assorted roasted vegetables can be the star of a dinner party, served with a simple dipping sauce like a tangy tahini or a vibrant chimichurri. Grilled vegetables can be tossed with pasta, layered in sandwiches, or used as a topping for pizzas and flatbreads.

Consider creating a roasted vegetable salad for a hearty main dish. Roast a mix of vegetables such as sweet potatoes, red onions, and Brussels sprouts. Once they are tender and caramelized, let them cool slightly before tossing with fresh arugula, toasted nuts, and a tangy vinaigrette. Add some crumbled feta or a handful of dried cranberries for extra flavor and texture.

For a Mediterranean-inspired meal, try grilling vegetables and serving them with a rich, creamy hummus. Grill eggplant, zucchini, and red peppers until nicely charred. Arrange them on a platter with a generous scoop of hummus, some olives, and warm pita bread. This makes for a delightful, shareable meal that's perfect for warm summer evenings.

Another fantastic option is to incorporate roasted or grilled vegetables into grain bowls. Start with a base of quinoa, farro, or brown rice. Add your choice of roasted vegetables, such as butternut squash, red onions, and cherry tomatoes. Top with a protein like chickpeas or tofu, and finish with a drizzle of tahini sauce or a sprinkle of nutritional yeast for a complete, balanced meal.

A particular favorite is roasted vegetable tacos. Roast a variety of vegetables, such as bell peppers, onions, and mushrooms, with a blend of spices like cumin, chili powder, and smoked paprika. Serve the roasted vegetables in warm tortillas with avocado, salsa, and a squeeze of lime. These tacos are not only delicious but also a fun way to enjoy a colorful, nutritious meal.

For those who enjoy a bit of sweetness, consider grilling fruits alongside your vegetables. Pineapple, peaches, and even watermelon can be grilled to bring out their natural sugars and add a caramelized touch. These grilled fruits pair wonderfully with savory vegetables and can be used in salads, salsas, or even desserts.

When planning a meal around roasted and grilled vegetables, think about the balance of flavors and textures. Combining different types of vegetables allows you to create a harmonious and varied dish. For example, pairing the sweetness of roasted carrots with the earthiness of grilled mushrooms and the slight bitterness of Brussels sprouts can create a well-rounded flavor profile. Adding a component with a contrasting texture, such as toasted nuts or seeds, can elevate the dish further.

Flavorful Rice and Grain Sides

Rice and grain sides are the unsung heroes of many meals, providing a flavorful and nutritious foundation that complements and even enhances the main dish. These versatile staples can be transformed into a myriad of dishes that are both exciting and satisfying. Understanding how to cook and season them properly can elevate your culinary repertoire, making every meal a delightful experience.

Starting with rice, the most common varieties are white, brown, basmati, and jasmine. Each type has its own unique texture and flavor profile, which can be further enhanced with the right cooking techniques and seasonings. White rice is the most neutral, making it a blank canvas for seasoning. A simple way to add flavor is to cook it in broth instead of water. Whether you use chicken, vegetable, or beef broth, this single step infuses the rice with a savory depth that plain water cannot provide.

For a more aromatic experience, consider using basmati or jasmine rice. These long-grain varieties have a natural fragrance that pairs beautifully with spices like cumin, cardamom, and cloves. To prepare, rinse the rice until the water runs clear to remove excess starch. This step ensures that the grains remain separate and fluffy. Sautéing the rice in a bit of oil with the spices before adding liquid can further enhance the flavor.

Brown rice, with its nutty flavor and chewy texture, is a whole grain that retains its bran and germ, making it more nutritious than white rice. It does take longer to cook, but the health benefits are worth it. To boost its flavor, try toasting the rice in a dry pan before cooking. This process brings out its natural nuttiness. You can also add bay leaves or a cinnamon stick to the cooking water for a subtle, aromatic touch.

Moving on to grains, quinoa has gained popularity due to its high protein content and versatility. Quinoa can be bland if not seasoned properly, so it's crucial to rinse it well before cooking to remove its natural saponin coating, which can be bitter. Cooking quinoa in broth and adding aromatics like garlic, onion, or ginger can make a significant difference. After cooking, fluff it with a fork and mix in fresh herbs, lemon zest, or a drizzle of olive oil for added flavor.

Farro, an ancient grain with a chewy texture and nutty taste, is another excellent option. It's perfect for hearty salads or as a side dish. Like brown rice, toasting farro before cooking enhances its flavor. Boil it in salted water or broth until tender, then drain any excess liquid. Tossing faro with roasted vegetables, feta cheese, and a splash of balsamic vinegar creates a robust and satisfying side.

Couscous, often mistaken for a grain, is actually a type of pasta made from semolina flour. It's incredibly quick and easy to prepare, making it ideal for weeknight dinners. To add flavor, cook couscous in broth and mix in sautéed onions, garlic, and spices like turmeric or paprika. Fluff it with a fork and fold in fresh herbs, dried fruits, or nuts for a burst of flavor and texture.

Bulgar wheat, made from cracked whole wheat kernels, is another versatile option. It has a slightly nutty flavor and a chewy texture. To prepare, simply soak it in hot water or broth until tender. Bulgar is the key ingredient in tabbouleh, a refreshing Middle Eastern salad. Mix it with chopped parsley, mint, tomatoes, and cucumbers, then dress with lemon juice and olive oil for a light and flavorful side.

Barley, a hearty grain with a chewy texture, is perfect for soups and stews but also makes a great side dish. Its natural sweetness pairs well with earthy vegetables and robust herbs. Cook barley in broth with bay leaves and thyme for added depth. Once cooked, mix it with roasted root vegetables and a drizzle of balsamic reduction for a comforting and nutritious side.

Millet, a small, round grain, is gluten-free and has a mild, slightly sweet flavor. It can be cooked to a fluffy or creamy consistency depending on the amount of liquid used. To bring out its flavor, toast millet in a dry skillet before cooking. Cook it in water or broth, then mix with sautéed vegetables, fresh herbs, and a squeeze of lemon juice for a light and flavorful side dish.

Experimenting with different grains and rice's opens up a world of culinary possibilities. Each grain has its own unique characteristics, and pairing them with complementary ingredients can result in remarkably flavorful and satisfying dishes. For instance, a wild rice blend cooked with mushrooms, onions, and garlic, then finished with a splash of soy sauce and toasted sesame seeds, offers a rich and savory side that pairs well with roasted meats or tofu.

For a Mediterranean-inspired dish, cook orzo, a rice-shaped pasta, in salted water until al dente. Drain and mix with sun-dried tomatoes, olives, feta cheese, and fresh basil. Dress with olive oil and lemon juice for a bright and tangy side that complements grilled fish or chicken.

Polenta, made from coarsely ground cornmeal, is another versatile side that can be served creamy or allowed to set and then grilled or fried. To make a creamy polenta, cook the cornmeal in water or broth, stirring frequently to prevent lumps. Once it has thickened, stir in butter and grated Parmesan cheese for a rich, savory flavor. For a unique twist, add roasted garlic or fresh herbs like rosemary or thyme. Alternatively, pour the cooked polenta into a baking dish, let it cool until firm, then cut into squares and grill or fry until golden and crispy. Serve with a tomato-based sauce or sautéed mushrooms for a delicious accompaniment.

Creative Potato Dishes

Potatoes, with their humble origins and versatile nature, are a staple in kitchens around the world. They can be transformed into an array of delightful dishes that satisfy both comfort food cravings and gourmet desires. The key to mastering creative potato dishes lies in understanding the varieties available and the cooking techniques that best highlight their unique textures and flavors.

Starting with the basics, potatoes come in several varieties, each suitable for different types of dishes. Russet potatoes, with their high starch content, are perfect for baking and mashing. Their fluffy texture when cooked makes them ideal for absorbing butter, cream, and other seasonings. For a classic baked potato, scrub the skin clean, pierce with a fork, and bake at 400°F until tender. Once done, a pat of salted butter and a sprinkle of chives can elevate this simple dish. For an indulgent twist, hollow out the baked potato, mix the insides with sour cream, cheese, and bacon, then return the mixture to the skins and bake again for a twice-baked delight.

Yukon Gold potatoes, known for their buttery flavor and smooth texture, are versatile and work well in both mashed and roasted forms. To make creamy mashed potatoes, boil peeled Yukon Golds until tender, then mash with warm milk, butter, and a touch of garlic. For an added layer of flavor, fold in roasted garlic or a sharp cheddar cheese. Roasting Yukon Golds is equally satisfying. Cut them into uniform pieces, toss with olive oil, salt, pepper, and rosemary, then roast at 425°F until golden and crispy. The result is a perfect side dish that pairs well with everything from roast chicken to grilled fish.

Red potatoes, with their waxy texture and thin skin, are excellent for salads and roasting. Their firm structure holds up well in a potato salad, where you can mix cooked, cubed red potatoes with a tangy dressing made from mayonnaise, Dijon mustard, apple cider vinegar, and fresh herbs like dill and parsley. Additions such as crispy bacon bits, chopped celery, and diced pickles can provide extra crunch and flavor. For a warm potato salad, toss roasted red potatoes with green beans, caramelized onions, and a mustard vinaigrette.

Fingerling potatoes, with their unique shapes and rich flavors, are perfect for gourmet dishes. Their small size makes them ideal for roasting whole. Toss them with olive oil, thyme, and sea salt, then roast until crispy. Serve them alongside grilled steak or as part of a charcuterie board. For an elegant appetizer, slice fingerlings lengthwise, roast until tender, then top with a dollop of crème fraiche and a spoonful of caviar or smoked salmon.

Sweet potatoes, while not botanically related to regular potatoes, offer a different spectrum of flavors and culinary opportunities. Their natural sweetness pairs well with both savory and sweet ingredients. For a savory dish, roast sweet potato wedges with a mix of cumin, paprika, and garlic powder. Serve with a yogurt dipping sauce spiked with lime juice and cilantro. For a sweet side, bake whole sweet potatoes until soft, then mash with brown sugar, cinnamon, butter, and a pinch of nutmeg. Top with toasted marshmallows or pecans for a holiday favorite.

Potato pancakes, or latkes, are a beloved dish in many cultures. Grating russet potatoes and mixing with grated onion, egg, and flour creates a batter that, when fried, turns into crispy, golden pancakes. Serve with applesauce and sour cream for a traditional take, or get creative with toppings like smoked salmon, avocado, or a poached egg.

Another innovative way to enjoy potatoes is by making gnocchi, a type of Italian dumpling. Start by baking russet potatoes until tender, then ricing them to a fine consistency. Mix with flour, egg, and a pinch of salt to form a dough. Roll the dough into ropes, cut into small pieces, and boil until they float. These pillow gnocchi can be sautéed with butter and sage or served with a rich tomato sauce.

Hassel back potatoes are a visually stunning dish that is surprisingly easy to make. Thinly slice russet or Yukon Gold potatoes without cutting all the way through, then brush with melted butter and season with salt and pepper. Bake until crispy on the outside and tender on the inside, basting with additional butter throughout the cooking process. For extra flavor, insert thin slices of garlic or cheese between the cuts before baking.

For a sophisticated twist on a classic, consider making a potato gratin. Thinly slice Yukon Gold potatoes and layer them in a baking dish with cream, garlic, and Gruyere cheese. Bake until the top is golden and bubbly, and the potatoes are tender. This rich and creamy dish is perfect for special occasions and pairs beautifully with roasted meats.

Potato soup is another comforting dish that can be both simple and elegant. Start with a base of sautéed leeks and onions, add diced potatoes and chicken or vegetable broth, and simmer until the potatoes are tender. Once the potatoes are tender, blend the soup until smooth for a creamy texture or leave some chunks for a more rustic feel. Stir in cream or milk for richness, and season with salt, pepper, and a touch of nutmeg. For a gourmet touch, garnish with crispy bacon bits, chives, and a swirl of crème fraîche. Alternatively, consider adding roasted garlic or a hint of truffle oil to the soup for an added layer of complexity.

Appetizers and Starters

The first course of any meal sets the tone for the culinary experience to follow. Appetizers and starters are more than just a prelude; they can be a showcase of creativity and flavor that excites the palate and whets the appetite. Crafting the perfect starter involves a balance of textures, flavors, and presentation, making it an art form in its own right.

Imagine welcoming guests to your home with a platter of vibrant bruschetta. This classic Italian appetizer is a simple yet elegant way to start a meal. Begin with a fresh baguette, sliced and lightly toasted. Rub each slice with a clove of garlic while still warm, then drizzle with high-quality extra virgin olive oil. The topping is where the magic happens: ripe tomatoes, finely diced, mixed with fresh basil, a splash of balsamic vinegar, and seasoned with salt and pepper. Spoon this mixture onto the toasted bread just before serving to maintain the perfect balance of crunch and juiciness. For an added layer of flavor, consider incorporating diced mozzarella or a sprinkle of Parmesan cheese.

Another crowd-pleaser is stuffed mushrooms. These bite-sized morsels can be filled with a variety of ingredients to suit different tastes. Start by removing the stems from button mushrooms and hollowing out the caps slightly. Sauté finely chopped mushroom stems with onions, garlic, and breadcrumbs until golden. Mix in grated Parmesan, chopped parsley, and a touch of cream cheese to bind it all together. Fill each mushroom cap with the mixture and bake until the mushrooms are tender and the tops are golden brown. These savory bites can be elevated with the addition of crumbled sausage, crab meat, or a sprinkle of truffle oil for a more luxurious twist.

For a lighter option, consider serving a platter of fresh spring rolls. These Vietnamese-inspired rolls are packed with crisp vegetables and fresh herbs, offering a refreshing start to any meal. Begin with rice paper wrappers, which need to be softened in warm water just before use. Fill each wrapper with a combination of julienned carrots, cucumbers, bell peppers, and fresh herbs like mint, basil, and cilantro. Adding shrimp, chicken, or tofu provides a protein boost. Roll them tightly and serve with a dipping sauce made from hoisin sauce, peanut butter, soy sauce, and a splash of lime juice. The contrast of crunchy vegetables and savory dipping sauce creates a delightful and healthy appetizer.

Cheese lovers will appreciate a well-curated cheese board. Select a variety of cheeses with different textures and flavors: a creamy brie, a sharp cheddar, a tangy blue cheese, and a hard, nutty Parmesan. Accompany the cheeses with an assortment of crackers, fresh fruits like grapes and apple slices, and nuts such as almonds and walnuts. Add a touch of sweetness with a small dish of honey or fig jam. The key to a successful cheese board is diversity, ensuring that there is something to please every palate. Arrange everything on a large wooden board or platter for an inviting and rustic presentation.

A Mediterranean-inspired appetizer that never fails to impress is baba ganoush. This smoky eggplant dip is perfect for serving with pita bread or fresh vegetables. Start by roasting a whole eggplant until the skin is charred and the flesh is soft. Once cooled, scoop out the flesh and blend it with tahini, garlic, lemon juice, and a drizzle of olive oil. Season with salt and a pinch of smoked paprika. The result is a creamy, flavorful dip that pairs beautifully with crunchy cucumber slices, bell pepper strips, and warm pita triangles.

For a more substantial starter, consider mini quiches. These can be made in a variety of flavors and are perfect for serving at a brunch or dinner party. Use store-bought or homemade pastry to line a mini muffin tin, then fill with a mixture of beaten eggs, cream, and your choice of fillings. Classic combinations include spinach and feta, bacon and cheddar, or mushroom and gruyere. Bake until the quiches are puffed and golden, and serve warm or at room temperature. These bite-sized quiches are not only delicious but also versatile, allowing you to cater to different dietary preferences with ease.

Seafood lovers will be delighted by the elegance of shrimp cocktail. This classic appetizer is simple yet sophisticated, making it a timeless favorite. Start by poaching large shrimp in a court bouillon made of water, white wine, lemon, bay leaves, and peppercorns. Once cooked and chilled, serve the shrimp with a tangy cocktail sauce made from ketchup, horseradish, lemon juice, and a dash of hot sauce. Arrange the shrimp on a bed of crushed ice with lemon wedges for a presentation that is both practical and visually appealing.

Another seafood option that brings a touch of elegance is smoked salmon canapés. Begin with small rounds of pumpernickel or rye bread, lightly toasted. Spread a thin layer of cream cheese on each round, then top with a slice of smoked salmon. Garnish with a sprig of fresh dill and a small dollop of capers or a slice of cucumber for a refreshing crunch. These canapés are not only visually appealing but also offer a perfect balance of creamy, smoky, and herbaceous flavors.

Dips, Spreads, and Tapas

When it comes to entertaining, dips, spreads, and tapas offer a delightful and versatile way to please a crowd. These small bites and shareable dishes are perfect for social gatherings, allowing guests to graze and mingle while enjoying a variety of flavors and textures. With just a bit of creativity and some basic ingredients, you can create a spread that leaves a lasting impression.

Imagine walking into a lively gathering, the air filled with the aroma of garlic and herbs, the sound of laughter mingling with clinking glasses. On the table, a vibrant array of dips and spreads await, inviting everyone to dive in. One of the stars of this display is a classic hummus, creamy and rich, made from blended chickpeas, tahini, olive oil, lemon juice, and garlic. The beauty of hummus lies in its adaptability; it can be flavored with roasted red peppers, sun-dried tomatoes, or a sprinkle of paprika for a bit of heat. Serve it with a selection of fresh vegetables, pita bread, or crispy lavash.

Alongside the hummus, consider the allure of a smoky baba ganoush. This Middle Eastern eggplant dip is both exotic and comforting. To make it, roast whole eggplants until the skins are charred and the flesh is tender. Scoop out the flesh and blend it with tahini, garlic, lemon juice, and a touch of cumin. The smokiness pairs beautifully with the creamy texture, making it a perfect companion to warm pita or crunchy crudités.

No spread is complete without a nod to Mediterranean flavors, and a vibrant tzatziki fits the bill perfectly. This refreshing Greek dip is made from thick Greek yogurt, minced garlic, grated cucumber, and fresh dill. A drizzle of olive oil and a squeeze of lemon juice round out the flavors. Tzatziki is not only delicious but also versatile, pairing well with grilled meats, vegetables, or simply as a cooling dip for bread.

For a taste of Spain, a platter of tapas can transport your guests to a bustling Spanish tavern. Start with patatas bravas, crispy fried potatoes served with a spicy tomato sauce and a drizzle of aioli. The contrast between the crispy potatoes and the creamy, spicy sauces is irresistible. Another tapas favorite is gambas al jabillo, or garlic shrimp. Sauté shrimp in olive oil with plenty of garlic, a touch of red pepper flakes, and a splash of white wine. Serve it sizzling hot with crusty bread to soak up the flavorful sauce.

A Spanish spread wouldn't be complete without a classic tortilla española, or Spanish omelet. This simple yet satisfying dish is made with thinly sliced potatoes and onions, slowly cooked in olive oil until tender, then mixed with beaten eggs and cooked until set. The result is a thick, hearty omelet that can be served warm or at room temperature, cut into wedges for easy sharing.

For a taste of Italy, consider a vibrant bruschetta. Start with slices of rustic bread, toasted until golden. Rub each slice with a clove of garlic while still warm, then top with a mixture of diced tomatoes, fresh basil, and a splash of balsamic vinegar. A sprinkle of salt and a drizzle of good olive oil complete this simple yet flavorful dish. For a twist, try topping the bruschetta with a variety of ingredients, such as creamy ricotta, roasted red peppers, or sautéed mushrooms.

Cheese spreads are another crowd-pleaser, and a well-made pimento cheese is a Southern classic that never fails to delight. This spread combines sharp cheddar cheese, mayonnaise, diced pimentos, and a touch of hot sauce for a creamy, tangy, and slightly spicy treat. Serve it with crackers, celery sticks, or even as a filling for finger sandwiches.

For a more exotic cheese spread, consider a herbed goat cheese. Mix soft goat cheese with a blend of fresh herbs such as chives, parsley, and thyme, along with a bit of lemon zest and black pepper. This spread is wonderfully tangy and fragrant, perfect for spreading on baguette slices or serving alongside roasted vegetables.

No gathering is complete without something a bit indulgent, and a warm spinach and artichoke dip fits the bill. This creamy, cheesy dip is made with a blend of cream cheese, sour cream, grated Parmesan, and mozzarella, mixed with chopped spinach and artichoke hearts. Bake until bubbly and golden, then serve with tortilla chips or sliced baguette for dipping.

A sweet and savory fig and olive tapenade offers a sophisticated twist on traditional spreads. Combine chopped black olives, dried figs, capers, garlic, and a splash of balsamic vinegar in a food processor, pulsing until finely chopped but still chunky. The result is a complex blend of sweet, salty, and tangy flavors that pairs beautifully with creamy cheeses or simply spread on crackers.

For a lighter option, a fresh guacamole is always a hit. Mash ripe avocados with lime juice, diced tomatoes, red onion, cilantro, and a bit of jalapeño for heat. Serve with tortilla chips or fresh vegetable sticks for a refreshing and satisfying dip. The creamy texture of the avocado combined with the brightness of the lime and the crunch of the onions creates a delightful balance that is both wholesome and delicious.

95

Chapter 6
Global Flavors

Italian Inspirations

The allure of Italian cuisine lies in its simplicity and the quality of its ingredients. Each dish tells a story, often rooted in tradition and passed down through generations. Italian cooking is not about complexity or extravagance but about bringing out the best in each ingredient. This chapter dives into the heart of Italian culinary traditions, offering practical advice and recipes to help you recreate these timeless dishes at home.

Picture a rustic kitchen in Tuscany, where the sun-drenched hills provide a backdrop to a meal lovingly prepared. The aroma of fresh basil, ripe tomatoes, and garlic fills the air. One of the cornerstones of Italian cuisine is the use of fresh, seasonal produce. Start with a simple yet iconic dish: Caprese salad. This classic salad features slices of ripe tomatoes, fresh mozzarella, and fragrant basil leaves, drizzled with extra virgin olive oil and a sprinkle of sea salt. The key to a perfect Caprese is the quality of the ingredients; choose the freshest tomatoes, the creamiest mozzarella, and the most aromatic basil you can find. This dish celebrates the flavors of summer and the simplicity of Italian cooking.

Moving to the realm of pasta, a staple in every Italian kitchen, there are countless varieties and sauces to explore. One of the most beloved is spaghetti carbonara, a dish that hails from Rome. The beauty of carbonara lies in its rich, creamy sauce made without cream. Instead, the sauce is crafted from beaten eggs, grated Pecorino Romano cheese, and pancetta. The heat from the freshly cooked pasta gently cooks the eggs, creating a silky, luscious coating. Be sure to use high-quality pancetta or guanciale, and freshly grated cheese for the best results. A generous grind of black pepper adds a final touch of spice, balancing the richness of the dish.

Another quintessential Italian pasta dish is Tagliatelle al Ragu, more commonly known outside Italy as Bolognese. This hearty meat sauce is a labor of love, simmered slowly to develop deep, complex flavors. Start with a soffritto of finely chopped onions, carrots, and celery, cooked gently in olive oil until soft and fragrant. Add ground beef and pork, browning the meat thoroughly before adding a splash of red wine. Once the wine has reduced, add tomatoes, a bay leaf, and a touch of milk to mellow the acidity. Let the sauce simmer for at least two hours, stirring occasionally. Serve it over fresh tagliatelle, a broad, flat noodle that holds the rich sauce beautifully.

No exploration of Italian cuisine would be complete without delving into risotto, a dish that embodies the essence of Italian comfort food. Risotto requires patience and attention, but the reward is a creamy, luxurious dish that is well worth the effort. A classic risotto alla Milanese is flavored with saffron, giving it a beautiful golden hue and a subtle, earthy flavor. Begin by sautéing finely chopped onions in butter until translucent. Add Arborio rice and toast it lightly, ensuring each grain is coated in butter. Gradually add hot chicken or vegetable broth, one ladle at a time, stirring constantly. This slow addition of liquid allows the rice to release its starches, creating a creamy texture. Stir in saffron threads steeped in a bit of warm broth, and finish with a generous handful of grated Parmesan cheese and a knob of butter for added richness.

Italian cuisine also shines in its bread and pizza offerings. Focaccia, a flat oven-baked bread, is a versatile and delicious addition to any meal. Its origins trace back to ancient Rome, and today, it remains a favorite across Italy. The dough is made with flour, water, yeast, salt, and olive oil, and it's typically topped with rosemary, sea salt, and more olive oil before baking. The result is a bread that is crispy on the outside, soft and airy on the inside, and infused with the flavors of olive oil and herbs. Focaccia can be enjoyed on its own, used as a sandwich bread, or served alongside soups and salads.

Pizza, perhaps Italy's most famous culinary export, varies greatly by region. The hallmark of a great pizza is a thin, crisp crust, achieved through high cooking temperatures and minimal toppings. A classic Margherita pizza, named after Queen Margherita of Savoy, features a simple topping of tomato sauce, fresh mozzarella, and basil, representing the colors of the Italian flag. The dough, made from flour, water, yeast, and salt, should be kneaded until smooth and elastic, then left to rise until doubled in size. Roll the dough out thinly, spread with tomato sauce, and top with slices of mozzarella and fresh basil leaves. Bake in a hot oven until the crust is golden and the cheese is bubbling. The simplicity of this pizza allows the quality of the ingredients to shine through, epitomizing the essence of Italian cooking.

Italian cuisine is also renowned for its desserts, with tiramisu being one of the most beloved. This coffee-flavored dessert is made by layering coffee -soaked ladyfingers with a rich mascarpone cheese mixture, then dusting with cocoa powder. The key to a perfect tiramisu lies in the balance of flavors and textures. Start by whisking egg yolks with sugar until pale and creamy, then fold in mascarpone cheese until smooth. In a separate bowl, whip the egg whites to stiff peaks and gently fold them into the mascarpone mixture. Dip ladyfingers briefly in strong coffee (and a splash of coffee liqueur if desired), then layer them in a dish, alternating with the mascarpone mixture. Chill the tiramisu for several hours to allow the flavors to meld and the texture to set. Just before serving, dust the top with unsweetened cocoa powder for a beautiful finish.

Asian Adventures

The vibrant and diverse flavors of Asian cuisine offer an adventure for the palate, inviting you to explore a world of spices, textures, and culinary techniques. Asian cooking is a symphony of flavors—sweet, sour, salty, and spicy—often harmonized in a single dish. The journey through Asian cuisine encompasses a vast array of regional specialties, each with its unique ingredients and methods. This chapter delves into the culinary traditions of various Asian countries, providing practical advice and recipes to help you bring these exotic flavors into your kitchen.

Imagine the bustling streets of Bangkok, where the air is filled with the tantalizing aromas of street food. One of the quintessential Thai dishes is Pad Thai, a stir-fried noodle dish that balances sweet, sour, salty, and spicy notes. To make an authentic Pad Thai, start with soaked rice noodles, which are stir-fried with eggs, tofu, shrimp, or chicken. The sauce, a blend of tamarind paste, fish sauce, palm sugar, and lime juice, is the heart of the dish. Garnish with crushed peanuts, fresh bean sprouts, and a wedge of lime. The key to perfect Pad Thai is to cook it quickly over high heat, ensuring the noodles are tender but not mushy, and the ingredients are well-coated with the flavorful sauce.

Moving to Japan, the art of sushi is a testament to the Japanese philosophy of simplicity and precision. Sushi, a dish that's as much about the quality of ingredients as the technique, begins with perfectly cooked and seasoned sushi rice. The rice is then combined with fresh fish, vegetables, and seaweed. There are various forms of sushi, from nigari (slices of fish atop small mounds of rice) to maki (rolls wrapped in seaweed). One of the most beloved types is the California roll, which combines crab meat, avocado, and cucumber. Mastering sushi requires practice and patience, but the result is a dish that's both visually stunning and delicious. Remember to use the freshest fish available and keep your knife sharp to achieve clean cuts.

In China, the diversity of regional cuisines is staggering, but one dish that has gained international acclaim is Peking duck. This Beijing specialty features a crispy-skinned duck served with thin pancakes, hoisin sauce, and scallions. The preparation of Peking duck is an art form, starting with air-drying the duck to achieve the signature crispy skin. The duck is then roasted until the skin is golden and the meat is tender. To serve, slice the duck thinly and wrap it in pancakes with a smear of hoisin sauce and a few slices of scallion. The combination of crispy skin, succulent meat, and savory sauce creates a mouthwatering experience.

Heading south to Vietnam, the cuisine is known for its fresh ingredients and balance of flavors. Pho, a fragrant noodle soup, is a cornerstone of Vietnamese cooking. The broth, made by simmering beef bones, star anise, cloves, and cinnamon, is the soul of the dish. Rice noodles, thinly sliced beef, bean sprouts, fresh herbs, and lime wedges are added just before serving. The result is a bowl of comfort that's aromatic and deeply satisfying. The secret to a great pho lies in the broth, which should be clear, richly flavored, and simmered slowly to extract maximum flavor from the bones and spices.

In India, the use of spices transforms simple ingredients into complex, flavorful dishes. One of the most popular Indian dishes is Chicken Tikka Masala, a dish that exemplifies the fusion of Indian and British culinary traditions. Marinated chicken pieces are grilled or baked until charred, then simmered in a creamy tomato sauce spiced with garam masala, cumin, coriander, and turmeric. The sauce is enriched with yogurt or cream, creating a rich, velvety texture. Serve Chicken Tikka Masala with basmati rice or naan bread to soak up the delicious sauce. The balance of smoky, spicy, and creamy flavors makes this dish a favorite around the world.

In the bustling markets of Seoul, Korea, street food offers a tantalizing array of flavors. One standout dish is Bibimbap, a mixed rice bowl topped with an array of vegetables, meat, and a fried egg. The dish is often seasoned with gochujang, a spicy red chili paste that adds depth and heat. To make Bibimbap, start with a base of steamed rice, and top with sautéed spinach, carrots, zucchini, shiitake mushrooms, and thinly sliced beef. Place a fried egg on top, and drizzle with sesame oil and gochujang. Mix everything together before eating to enjoy a symphony of flavors and textures in each bite.

In Malaysia, the influence of Chinese, Indian, and Malay cuisines creates a vibrant culinary landscape. Laksa, a spicy noodle soup, is a beloved dish that reflects this cultural melting pot. There are many variations of laksa, but one popular version is the curry laksa. It features a rich, coconut-based broth spiced with lemongrass, turmeric, and galangal. The broth is poured over rice noodles and topped with shrimp, tofu puffs, bean sprouts, and hard-boiled eggs. Garnish with fresh cilantro, lime wedges, and sambal (chili paste) for an extra kick. The combination of creamy coconut, aromatic spices, and fresh toppings makes laksa a comforting and satisfying dish that captures the essence of Malaysian cuisine.

Mexican Fiesta

The heart and soul of Mexican cuisine lie in its rich history, vibrant colors, and bold flavors. A traditional Mexican fiesta is not just about eating; it is a celebration of culture, family, and heritage. From the aromatic spices to the timeless cooking techniques, each dish tells a story of the land and its people. Preparing a Mexican feast at home requires a love for fresh ingredients, a bit of patience, and an adventurous spirit. This chapter will guide you through the essentials of creating an unforgettable Mexican fiesta, complete with practical advice and recipes that even beginners can master.

Imagine the bustling markets of Oaxaca, where the scent of fresh tortillas mingles with the earthy aroma of dried chilies. One of the most beloved staples in Mexican cuisine is the humble tortilla, a versatile base for many dishes. Freshly made corn tortillas are a revelation compared to their store-bought counterparts. To make them at home, you need masa harina, a type of corn flour treated with lime. Mix it with water to form a dough, then press it into thin rounds using a tortilla press. Cook the tortillas on a hot griddle until they puff slightly and develop a few charred spots. Serve them warm, and use them as a base for tacos, enchiladas, or simply enjoy them with a pat of butter and a sprinkle of salt.

Tacos al pastor, a popular street food, showcases the fusion of Mexican and Middle Eastern flavors. This dish features marinated pork, traditionally cooked on a vertical spit similar to shawarma. At home, you can achieve similar results using a grill or oven. Marinate thinly sliced pork in a mixture of achiote paste, pineapple juice, vinegar, and spices like cumin and oregano. Skewer the marinated pork and grill until it's tender and slightly charred. Serve the meat on warm corn tortillas, topped with diced onions, fresh cilantro, and a squeeze of lime. The combination of smoky, tangy, and savory flavors makes tacos al pastor a crowd-pleaser.

No Mexican fiesta is complete without guacamole, a creamy avocado dip that's incredibly easy to make. Start with ripe avocados, mashing them to your desired consistency. Add finely chopped red onion, fresh cilantro, diced tomatoes, and a squeeze of lime juice. Season with salt and, if you like a bit of heat, add some chopped jalapeño. Serve guacamole with tortilla chips or use it as a topping for tacos and enchiladas. The key to great guacamole is using fresh ingredients and balancing the flavors to let the avocado shine.

For a hearty main course, consider making mole polao, a rich and complex sauce from the state of Puebla. Mole combines a multitude of ingredients, including dried chilies, spices, nuts, seeds, and even chocolate. The sauce is traditionally served over chicken or turkey. To make mole polao, toast and rehydrate a variety of dried chilies such as ancho, pasilla, and mulato. Blend the chilies with roasted tomatoes, onions, garlic, and a mixture of spices including cinnamon, cloves, and cumin. Add ground nuts and seeds for thickness, and a bit of Mexican chocolate for depth. Simmer the sauce until it's thick and velvety, then pour it over cooked poultry. The result is a dish that's both savory and slightly sweet, with layers of flavor that develop with each bite.

Tamales are another classic dish that embodies the communal spirit of Mexican cooking. These steamed corn dough parcels can be filled with various ingredients, from shredded chicken in a green chili sauce to sweet corn and raisin mixtures. Making tamales is often a family affair, with multiple generations gathering to prepare and assemble them. To make tamales, start by preparing a masa dough with masa harina, lard or vegetable shortening, and broth. Spread the dough onto soaked corn husks, add your filling, and fold the husks to encase the dough. Steam the tamales until the dough is firm and cooked through. Serve them with salsa or mole for a comforting and satisfying meal.

No fiesta would be complete without a refreshing beverage, and horchata is a popular choice. This creamy rice drink is flavored with cinnamon and vanilla, and it's perfect for cooling down on a hot day. To make horchata, soak white rice with cinnamon sticks in water overnight. Blend the mixture until smooth, then strain it through a fine-mesh sieve to remove any solids. Sweeten with sugar and add a splash of vanilla extract. Serve chilled over ice for a delightful, refreshing drink that pairs well with spicy dishes.

For dessert, churros con chocolate are a must-try. These crispy, fried dough pastries are coated in cinnamon sugar and served with a rich chocolate dipping sauce. To make churros, prepare a dough with flour, water, butter, and a pinch of salt. Pipe the dough into hot oil, frying until golden brown and crisp. Roll the churros in a mixture of cinnamon and sugar while they're still warm. For the chocolate sauce, melt dark chocolate with a bit of cream and a touch of cinnamon. The combination of crispy churros and velvety chocolate makes for a decadent end to your Mexican feast.

Taste of the Mediterranean

Sun-drenched landscapes, azure waters, and a culinary heritage that spans millennia—these elements define the Mediterranean region. The Mediterranean diet, renowned for its health benefits, is a celebration of seasonal produce, fresh herbs, and simple yet flavorful preparations. This chapter will delve into the vibrant tapestry of Mediterranean cuisine, offering practical guidance and recipes to help you bring the essence of this storied region to your kitchen.

Picture a bustling market in Sicily, where vendors enthusiastically peddle plump tomatoes, fragrant basil, and glistening olive oil. The Mediterranean diet thrives on such fresh ingredients, and one of its most iconic dishes is the Caprese salad. To create this quintessential Italian starter, arrange thick slices of ripe tomatoes and fresh mozzarella on a platter. Tuck basil leaves between the layers, then drizzle with extra virgin olive oil and a splash of balsamic vinegar. Sprinkle with sea salt and freshly ground black pepper. The result is a dish that marries the sweetness of tomatoes with the creamy texture of mozzarella and the herbal notes of basil, all elevated by the olive oil's fruitiness.

Moving eastward, the shores of Greece offer another cornerstone of Mediterranean cuisine: Greek salad.

Known locally as horiatiki, this salad is a symphony of crunchy vegetables and briny accents. Combine chunks of cucumber, ripe tomatoes, green bell pepper, red onion, and Kalamata olives in a bowl. Add generous cubes of feta cheese and dress with a simple mixture of extra virgin olive oil, red wine vinegar, dried oregano, and a pinch of salt. Serve immediately to enjoy the crisp textures and contrasting flavors.

No Mediterranean meal is complete without bread, and few are as beloved as focaccia from Italy. This flatbread, with its golden crust and airy interior, is easy to make at home. Begin by dissolving yeast in warm water, then mix with flour, salt, and olive oil to form a dough. Allow it to rise until doubled in size. Press the dough into a baking sheet, dimple the surface with your fingers, and drizzle generously with olive oil. Sprinkle with coarse sea salt and fresh rosemary. Bake until the focaccia is golden and crisp. Serve warm, perhaps with a small dish of olive oil and balsamic vinegar for dipping.

The Mediterranean Sea's bounty is not limited to its produce; it is also rich in seafood. A classic example is Spanish paella, a dish that originated in Valencia. Paella combines rice with a variety of seafood, meat, and vegetables, all cooked in a single pan. To make paella, start by sautéing onions, garlic, and bell peppers in olive oil. Add short-grain rice and stir to coat the grains. Pour in a mixture of chicken broth and saffron threads, then nestle in pieces of chicken, chorizo, and an assortment of seafood like shrimp, mussels, and clams. Cook until the rice is tender and the liquid is absorbed. Garnish with fresh parsley and lemon wedges before serving. The layers of flavor in paella—from the smoky chorizo to the sweet seafood—make it a dish that is both comforting and celebratory.

From the Levant, we find another beloved Mediterranean staple: hummus. This creamy chickpea dip is both nutritious and versatile. To make authentic hummus, blend cooked chickpeas with tahini, lemon juice, garlic, and a splash of olive oil. Season with salt and, for a bit of heat, a dash of cayenne pepper. Serve hummus with warm pita bread or fresh vegetables. For a twist, top it with a drizzle of olive oil, a sprinkle of paprika, or even some toasted pine nuts.

Lamb, another Mediterranean favorite, finds its pinnacle in dishes like Moroccan lamb tagine. This slow-cooked stew is named after the earthenware pot in which it is traditionally prepared. Start by browning lamb chunks in olive oil, then remove them from the pan. Sauté onions, garlic, and ginger until fragrant, then add spices such as cumin, coriander, cinnamon, and turmeric. Return the lamb to the pot along with chopped tomatoes, dried apricots, and a bit of chicken broth. Cover and simmer until the lamb is tender and the flavors have melded. Serve the tagine over couscous, garnished with fresh cilantro and toasted almonds. The interplay of sweet and savory elements, coupled with the rich spices, makes this dish a memorable centerpiece for any meal.

Vegetables play a starring role in Mediterranean cuisine, and one of the most beloved preparations is ratatouille from France. This Provençal dish uses summer's bounty of vegetables, including eggplant, zucchini, bell peppers, and tomatoes. Begin by sautéing each type of vegetable separately in olive oil to ensure they retain their individual textures and flavors. Then, combine them in a large pot with garlic, onions, and fresh herbs like thyme and basil. Simmer gently until the flavors meld together. Ratatouille can be served hot or at room temperature, as a side dish or a light main course, often accompanied by crusty bread to soak up the flavorful juices. The key to an excellent ratatouille lies in the quality of the vegetables and the patience to cook them slowly, allowing their natural sweetness to develop and mingle.

Comfort Food from Around the World

The scent of freshly baked bread, the warmth of a hearty stew, the satisfaction of a well-spiced curry—comfort food is a universal language that speaks to our need for nourishment, both physical and emotional. Each culture has its own cherished dishes that offer solace and a sense of home. This chapter explores a selection of comforting dishes from around the globe, each with its unique story and culinary tradition.

Imagine a cold winter's evening in a quaint English village. The wind howls outside, but inside, a bubbling pot of shepherd's pie promises warmth and comfort. This classic dish, traditionally made with minced lamb (or beef, in which case it is often called cottage pie), is a staple in British cuisine. To prepare shepherd's pie, start by cooking ground lamb with onions, carrots, and peas. Season with Worcestershire sauce, thyme, and a hint of rosemary. Spread the mixture in a baking dish and top with a generous layer of creamy mashed potatoes. Bake until the top is golden and crispy. The result is a hearty, savory dish that warms you from the inside out.

Traveling to France, we encounter another beloved comfort food: coq au vin. This rich, flavorful stew dates back to ancient Gaul and has become a symbol of rustic French cooking. To make coq au vin, marinate chicken pieces in red wine, garlic, and herbs overnight. The next day, brown the chicken in a large pot, then sauté onions, garlic, and mushrooms in the same pot. Return the chicken to the pot along with the marinade, some chicken broth, and a bouquet garni. Simmer until the chicken is tender and the flavors have melded together. Serve coq au vin with crusty bread or buttery mashed potatoes to soak up the delicious sauce. The deep, complex flavors of this dish make it a favorite for special occasions and family gatherings alike.

In Italy, comfort food often means a steaming plate of pasta. One of the most iconic and beloved dishes is lasagna. Layers of pasta, rich meat sauce, creamy béchamel, and melted cheese come together in a symphony of flavors and textures. To prepare lasagna, start by making a meat sauce with ground beef, tomatoes, onions, garlic, and Italian herbs like basil and oregano. In a separate pot, prepare a béchamel sauce with butter, flour, and milk. Begin layering in a baking dish: start with a thin layer of meat sauce, followed by a layer of pasta, then béchamel, and a sprinkle of grated Parmesan. Repeat the layers, finishing with a generous topping of mozzarella cheese. Bake until bubbly and golden. Lasagna is a dish that brings families together, often prepared for Sunday dinners and holidays.

Moving eastward, we find ourselves in the heart of Russia, where borscht is a beloved comfort food. This vibrant beet soup is a staple in Russian and Eastern European cuisine. Borscht can be enjoyed hot or cold, but the hot version is especially comforting in the colder months. To make borscht, start by sautéing onions, carrots, and celery in a large pot. Add diced beets, potatoes, and cabbage, then pour in beef or vegetable broth. Simmer until the vegetables are tender. Finish with a splash of vinegar and a dollop of sour cream. The deep, earthy flavor of the beets, combined with the tang of the vinegar and the creaminess of the sour cream, makes borscht a deeply satisfying dish.

Crossing the Atlantic, we land in the southern United States, home to one of the ultimate comfort foods: fried chicken. Crispy on the outside, juicy on the inside, fried chicken is a dish that brings people together. To make classic Southern fried chicken, marinate chicken pieces in buttermilk overnight. This tenderizes the meat and infuses it with flavor. The next day, dredge the chicken in a seasoned flour mixture, ensuring each piece is well-coated. Fry in hot oil until golden brown and crispy. Serve with sides like mashed potatoes, gravy, and coleslaw. Fried chicken is often associated with family gatherings, picnics, and celebrations, making it a true comfort food.

In Japan, comfort food takes the form of ramen, a noodle soup that has captured the hearts and stomachs of people around the world. A bowl of ramen consists of four key components: broth, noodles, toppings, and tare (seasoning). The broth can be made from pork, chicken, or vegetables and is simmered for hours to develop a rich, deep flavor. To prepare a basic ramen, start by making the broth with bones, onions, garlic, ginger, and Kombu (dried kelp). Cook the noodles separately until just tender. Assemble the ramen by placing the noodles in a bowl, ladling over the hot broth, and adding toppings like sliced pork, soft-boiled eggs, nori (seaweed), and green onions. A good ramen is a balance of flavors and textures, offering comfort and satisfaction with every slurp. Another Asian comfort food that deserves mention is Thailand's famous curry, particularly green curry. This aromatic dish is both spicy and soothing, providing a perfect balance of heat and comfort. To prepare green curry, start by making or purchasing green curry paste, which typically includes ingredients like green chilies, garlic, lemongrass, kaffir lime leaves, and galangal. Sauté the curry paste in a pot with a bit of oil until fragrant. Add coconut milk and bring to a simmer. Then, add sliced chicken, eggplant, and bamboo shoots. Allow the curry to cook until the chicken is tender and the vegetables are cooked through. Finish with Thai basil and a splash of fish sauce for depth of flavor.